A HAPPIER FAMILY

FACING
TEN COMMON CAUSES
OF FAMILY FAILURE

A HAPPIER FAMILY

FACING TEN COMMON CAUSES OF FAMILY FAILURE

by
MARGOT
HOVER, D.Min.

Cover and interior design and art by Ron Fendel

Library of Congress Catalog Card Number 77-90163
ISBN 0-89622-074-5

Typeset and printed in the United States of America.

Contents

Introduction

Item: A favorite theology professor of mine used to say that the world's best theologian is Goldie Hawn, precisely because her standard question is, "What's it all about?"

Item: According to Richard Levy and Roger Langley, authors of *Wifebeating,* 28 million American women—one half of the married women in the United States—are the victims of assault within the home. Ten percent of those incidents involve lethal weapons.

Item: Recently, I spent some time with a diocesan director of education, discussing possible approaches for a set of workshops I was conducting for parents. "Your ideas are fine," he said, "but for heaven's sake, don't mention psychology. That will really upset them."

Item: Government figures for 1975 predicted that one-third of recent first marriages will end in divorce. During 1976, that rate increased by more than four percent.

When I first went into parish work, family was **not** an issue. I can still remember Confirmation that year, beginning with the bishop's visit to the parish staff on the afternoon of the service. He looked sternly at me over his glasses, pointing a sharp finger in my direction as he reminded me that the parish census figures declared our teenaged population to be in the neighborhood of 150 while attendance at our religious education programs was closer to 40. I remember feeling that my ship was sinking. He stared into space as I tried to explain that our approach included a number of family options, in which some of those students were participating.

No sale! But youth programs sometimes seemed to me to pose more problems than they solved. I was intrigued with the possibility of designing an approach that would more effectively integrate religious operations and family living, using tools from psychology and sociology as well as theology.

And so the next year, I began a full scale study of the nature of family religious awareness. I worked through the medium of a bi-weekly newsletter which my colleague, Dr. Monica Breidenbach, and I wrote for three years. *Seeds for Family Living* eventually reached 1000 families, as subscribers heard about it from relatives and friends.

I suppose that as I began my research, I assumed that these people had the following traits. First, they were deeply committed to their families. After all, they were reading our newsletter about family religious celebrations and communication techniques, and an amazing number of them frequently wrote back to comment on our work and to share their insights.

Second, I assumed that they were stable. Everybody knows that "The family that prays together stays together," and has fewer catastrophes. Since I was concentrating on content at that point, I wanted to try out my ideas on families that would be untouched by upheavals. Third, I felt that these people would be fairly unsophisticated in their theological understandings.

During my study, I modified those assumptions. These families were indeed deeply committed to working at being families. Depending largely on their religious affiliation—some denominations inculcate a more narrow view of family ministry than others—they were glad to be supported in their hunch that clearer communication and more honest family dynamics could be tools for religious discovery. They became increasingly more aware of those moments in family living which form religious values, and more at ease in celebrating them together. And I became convinced of their ability to theologize and communicate with each other.

But they were not free of upheavals. During one two-year period, there were deaths both of family members and of marriages. Conflicts surfaced. Roles were redefined and exchanged, with more struggle and expended energy than any of us dreamed it would take. "Crisis?" a subscriber replied in answer to one survey. "Take summer, for example. The whole season is a crisis!"

So I discovered a lot about families as these generous people shared themselves with us. And I asked Goldie Hawn's question myself. What **is** it all about? I learned that theology is the accumulated reflection of persons on their relationship with God. I already knew the value of church tradition and the insights of earlier searchers as challenge and verification of my insights, but I became convinced of the primacy of my own experience as a starting point in my search.

My own theology shifted from the static terms I had learned earlier to an understanding of faith as the continual risk of acknowledging a center of meaning greater than myself. Any risk is difficult but the risk of faith is impossible if one views oneself as being at the mercy of a capricious and uninvolved God, Who holds us in the palm of His hand but drops us occasionally for the good of our souls. My faith is a risk of strength because it is always difficult both to rely on the intangible, and to let go of my imagined self-sufficiency. But it is enabled by grace, the free gift of God's life and love. I believe that it is mine for the asking because I believe the witness of Christ.

The tools I selected from the area of psychology were taken from those contemporary schools of thought that emphasize the imperative of considering people as beings who are able to take charge of their lives, who are thus able to make commitments. Further, the modern approach to people in the context of their whole existence, including their relationships with others, was made to order for my study.

Perhaps because we know more about family systems now, we are also more aware of the ways in which we can promote healthy, growth-producing family relationships. Moreover, it seemed clear to me that to the extent that tools for psychological growth enable us to trust and to enter into relationships, they are tools for growth in religious awareness.

Sociology is the study of the milieu in which theological reflection and psychological analysis of behavior take place. It was this field that convinced me that the families of my study weren't unusual. Sociologists proved statistically that the family is where communication of values really takes place, despite assumptions of school systems to the contrary. Sociologists revealed that even if a Dick-Jane-Spot-Father-Mother family ever did exist, it is no longer reliable to assume that it exists now.

So what is it all about? We all learned that to be religious is not to have eliminated all life's compartments except the one in which we go to church on Sunday, sit in the front pew, use the collection envelope, and stay awake during the sermon. It isn't even to donate to the doorbell-ringing Cancer Fund lady because "There but for the grace of God. . .". To be religious is to see that there is no compartment that is not religious. It is to realize that it is by being social, psychological, physical, emotional and moral beings that we reach God, and then to discover that we are not "reaching" God, but finding Presence where it has been all the time, in the center of our being. In that sense, holiness is wholeness.

It follows then, that it is religious activity to deal with the compartments, the dichotomies. The religious person is truly one who is "getting it all together." To look at our lives, our values, our relationships clearly and carefully and to deal with what in them is a source of division is religious activity. It is religious activity to examine the real reasons why I "tolerate" my parents, nag my husband, ignore my wife, disparage my children. It is religious activity to explore ways of dealing with the feelings that we are usually content to let fester and the compliments and thank you's we are uncomfortable giving.

The paradox is that until we have done that work, theological formulae are crutches. To the extent that we pursue our creeds and our churches to keep from looking at the "weekday" parts of our lives, we make it impossible to find real meaning. Again, wholeness is not denying the various compartments; it is dealing with them so that they can be integrated into the whole.

And that's what this book is all about. "Oh, you mean that this is therapy that a regular family can do for itself," exclaimed one of my neighbors when I explained this project to her. Well, my goal is to offer to families a variety of ways of dealing with their living together. These units focus on sources of considerable tension for couples **and/or** families, with suggested activities that involve them in taking charge of the situation. There is no reason for us to be victims of the circumstances in which we find ourselves, and there is also no reason why all members of the family shouldn't lend their gifts to the process.

The chapters of this book are grouped as they deal with the basic components of family relationships (inner workings), family organization patterns, the family and society, and the family's religious values system.

Each chapter begins with a brief case study or real-life example. This is followed by some provocative questions to help the reader (hopefully you and your spouse) to focus on essential aspects. The theory for and dealing with analyzing the specific problem follows and the Familylab with its concrete method ends the chapter. The Familylab is a workshop for you to do with your spouse and if possible, with your children. Beware of discounting the contributions of younger children. They're part of your daily living, and can be a part of these sessions. And don't be too quick to say that these won't work for **your** family. All it takes is a commitment to the process.

Following each section is an annotated bibliography of

books for further reading. The list is not intended to be exhaustive, of course, and you will probably disagree with some sections of some of the books. Nevertheless, all of them present at least a point of departure for your own thinking.

Simply because this book is about human relationships, it goes without saying that many people played a part in its composition. There are all of the families I've encountered as a Director of Religious Education, workshop director, and counselor. There are the families in Columbus, Ohio, who regularly welcomed me into their homes and enriched me by their sharing. There is the special group of parents who worked with me and with each other during my years of research on family religious awareness and communication. The incredible openness of these people had a great effect on my notions of family dynamics, and their continuing support and friendship have enabled me to attempt and complete projects like this book. My convictions about the richness and complexity of family relationships began with my supportive and creative parents. In a special way, however, this book flows from my friendship with Dr. Monica Breidenbach and our relationship of mutual challenge and support. She worked with me to develop and test the Familylabs. She listened as I thought aloud about the various theories. But most of all, her spirit makes our home a very good place to be.

PART ONE

FAMILY DYNAMICS

Chapter 1

Communication Patterns

Judy: I hate soup. I'm not going to eat this. You always cook yucky food, and I'm not going to eat it.   (Child)*

Mother: I don't like it when you say things like that. I feel like running away, and then you'll have to cook your own yucky food for yourself.   (Child)

Judy: That's dumb. You know that mothers shouldn't run away and leave their kids. (Parent)

Mother: And children aren't supposed to talk back to their parents, either.   (Parent)

Judy: Well, why can't we pick out what kind of soup we want for lunch? That way, I would pick out the kind I like.   (Adult)

Mother: You mean that you would eat it, if you had a chance to choose the kind you want each day? All right, we'll do that beginning tomorrow.   (Adult)

1. *Do many of your family conversations end up as shouting matches?*

2. *Do you ever feel "put down" in family transactions?*

3. *Have you sometimes had the feeling that a transaction has gone wrong even though you began with the best and clearest intentions?*

4. *Is it difficult to get others to understand what you mean?*

5. *Do you find yourself responding to others in ways that increase conflict or cause relationships to deteriorate?*

Communication refers to the process of giving and receiving meaning. Transactions include both verbal and nonverbal signs with a wide variety of symbols and clues that enrich and specify the message sent and received. For example, "Mommy, Carl is chasing me," Julie complains, although she shrieks with delight as the chase resumes. "Hello, dear; I missed you today," Marie says to her husband as she dries her hands and leaves the kitchen to kiss him at the front door. "If you had hired a lawn service last fall, you wouldn't be having such difficulty with your grass now," declares a neighbor, standing with hand on hip and punctuating his sentence by poking the air with his index finger.

Communication is necessary for survival. We need information about the world, and we need to know about other people and the ways in which they perceive us and relate to each other and to us. What behaviors does society consider acceptable? What actions win approval in the family setting? How do you get to the nearest store from here? Whose turn is it to do the dishes tonight? Yes, communication is vital.

But communication is difficult. In the first place, words themselves are often ambiguous. For example, "I was only a **little** late," says Alex. "Act your age," warns Mary's mother. "How do I look, dear?" Joan asks her husband. "You already know the answer to that question!" Jim snaps to his son. "He

---

*Parenthetical distinctions are explained as terms of Transactional Analysis on the following pages.

isn't very . . . **you** know," confides Jill to her girlfriend. In each case, there is a strong possibility that the message received by the listener is not clear.

Nonverbal clues may help the listener to discover a precise meaning or pinpoint the emotional climate in which the transaction was made. Alex may look apologetic or defiant. Mary's mother points her finger and scowls. Joan is poised with expectancy of an approving evaluation from her husband. Jim fixes his son with an icy stare. Jill accompanies her statement with a raised eyebrow. Communication is like putting the pieces of a puzzle together.

In the second place, communication is a gamble. There is the danger that my message will be misunderstood. For example, "The latest issue of *Camper's Journal* says that Disney World is a great place for a vacation," I idly comment to my wife. "Don't tell me that you've changed your mind again!" she wails. "This year we were going to do what I wanted to do." And of course, the perennial, "Mommy, where did I come from?" which may merit an "Ask your father," or a two-hour illustrated lecture before anyone thinks to check out the meaning of the child's question.

And finally, I may feel that I am communicating thoroughly and clearly only to have an exchange fail completely. What happened? Our behavior is a reflection of one of the three ego positions that compose our personality in the Transactional Analysis schema. In the language of TA, each person enters a conversation as Parent, Child or Adult. None of these is related to chronological age or family position; children have a very active Parent side and indulging the Child can be a source of growth for all adults, for example.

So both sender and receiver of a message bring to the exchange their own mind set. When we engage in communication with other people, their responses proceed from their Parent, Adult or Child positions, just as ours do. For example, what may seem to me to be a simple request for information may elicit an angry response because I was heard by an unexpected part of the other's personality. "Where are my tennis shoes?" my Adult asks my wife. "If you'd put them away where they belong, you would know," her Parent snaps. "How much is this car?" my Adult asks the automobile salesman. "If you have to ask, you can't afford it," replies his Parent.

All three personality states are signaled by physical and verbal clues that reveal which one is in action at the moment. Typically, the Parent has a wrinkled forehead, a pointed index finger, one hand on hip, or one hand poised to pat someone on the head. In addition, there are patterns which the Parent has borrowed from the biological parents. One person may, "Tsk! Tsk!" in the Parent state; another may tap a foot or sigh exaggeratedly. Verbal clues that the Parent is in operation include "always" and "never," as well as a host of evaluative terms that have little basis in measurable fact. The Parent makes such statements as, "Never speak to strangers;" "That kind of behavior is disgusting;" and "Smoking ought to be outlawed." The Adult may agree after investigating the issue, but it is the habitual use of these statements that indicates the Parent as their source.

The Child, too, sends its signals. Most of the Child's cues are nonverbal: tears, giggling, squealing, pouting, slouching, and nosethumbing, for example. But there are verbal signs as well: for example, bragging and babytalk, as well as many "I wish" and "I want" statements. Both the Child and the Parent have benefits and liabilities for us. The Parent can be loving and protective, and the Child can be recalcitrant as well as engaging.

The Adult, the decision maker, is an intent, thorough listener. When the Adult speaks, that ego position asks fact questions in order to get information necessary for those decisions. For example, "I really would like to know the price of this car," insists the adult to the scornful auto salesman. Statements are qualified in contrast to the generalization of the other two ego states. For example, "It is my opinion that high-school students should be allowed to vote," is quite different from, "High school students should definitely be allowed to vote!" on the one hand, and "Darn! they never get to do **any**thing!" on the other.

Complementary transactions occur when a message sent from one ego state is responded to from the expected ego state of the other. For example, "I have an awful headache," my Child complains to my husband's Parent. "You've been working too hard today; I'll do the dishes while you put your feet up," his Parent responds sympathetically. Nice! "Do I have time to change my clothes before supper?" my husband's Adult asks. "You'll have about 10 minutes," my Adult replies. "Kids today have terrible manners," says my Parent. "That's exactly right," agrees my wife's Parent.

The following diagrams indicate these typical complementary transactions:

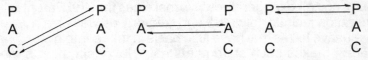

All of these transactions are "successful" in the sense that they can continue. In the preceding examples, the Adult request for information receives an Adult factual reply. The Parent judgment is supported by an agreeing Parent judgment. And the Child asks for and receives some Parent sympathy. Whether the transaction is appropriate is another question. Eventually, my Child may tire of being parented or the playmate may want to have a turn at being Parent. Eric Berne's *Games People Play* is a description of complementary transactions that are inappropriate or that players resort to as a way of avoiding honesty and intimacy with each other.

In the setting of the family, difficulties often arise over crossed transactions. I send a message to one ego state and another ego state cuts in. For example, my Adult asks my wife's Adult if she can drop off the car at the service station. But her Child responds to my Parent: "I don't see why I have to do everything. Today I have to do the washing, make the potato salad for the office picnic, take Jerry in to have his braces adjusted, and now you want me to go to the garage with the car!" The transaction looks like this:

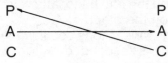

"Dad, I can't stand that stupid school any longer; I'm going to drop out next semester," says my 16-year-old son's Child, in hopes of engaging my Parent. A Parent response would be either, "No son of mine is going to be an illiterate bum," or, "You're right; they aren't being very nice to you, are they." Instead, my Adult may answer, "You're really upset about school?"

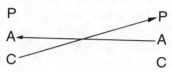

A crossed transaction cannot continue on the footing intended by the initiating person. In the first example, that's a problem; in the second, that's a help. One of the advantages of Active Listening ("Listening" Chapter 2) is that it helps the other person to express all of the Child and Parent feelings that are obscuring a clear and rational examination of an issue so that the Adult is free to focus on it.

Thus, if instead of responding to my son from my Parent, I put my Adult in gear, he will probably talk out his feelings of anger, frustration or boredom. At that point, his Adult may decide that he is too close to graduation to quit now. Or his Adult may decide that there are other ways of completing his education, or even that he would like to take his chances without a diploma. In any event, it clearly will be his decision. If I respond from my Parent, his decision will probably proceed from his Child ("I know how to make you really mad," or "Parents know best."). If things don't work out for him as he expected, he will probably again lapse into his Child to blame me for the failure.

Active Listening is effective in helping people of all ages to make decisions from their Adult. For example, "Mommy, Janie is picking on me," my four-year-old wails, pulling out all the stops on her Child. My Parent may respond with either "Well, I'll fix her," or "Big girls don't whine," or my own Child may wail back, "How can I get all of my work done when you keep bothering me!" Or my Adult can reply, "You're tired of playing with her?" or "You wish she wouldn't tease you?" The latter responses encourage her to talk about her bruised feelings, but the responsibility for dealing with Janie is still hers. Ultimately, once she has talked about her feelings until she is satisfied, she will know how to take care of the situation herself.

Ideally, family members want to be free to operate from any of the three states as each particular situation demands. Everyone suffers when family communication patterns solidify to the point that members are free to express only one or two of the states. With family roles in our society in such flux, this is a source of great tension. Women are experimenting with assertiveness more readily than men are willing to relinquish their old position as chief providers and family protectors, for example. In other words, women are trying out their Adult, while their husbands are often still operating primarily out of their Parent in the family arena. "One of the hardest things about going back to school (attending human development classes, going back to work) is that it threatens my husband," is the theme that so many wives express.

Ironically, however, if retreating to a single pattern is safe and risk-free, it also has its eventual drawbacks. The husband who can respond only as Parent will probably grow to resent the burden of responsibility he bears alone. The wife who is comfortable only as Child will wonder why no one takes her seriously when she attempts Adult transactions. Children who act only out of their Child will perennially blame others for their own decisions, and will miss the warmth that comes from occasionally nurturing others, even when they are one's own parents.

This Familylab offers some exercises for examining together the relationships that are characteristic of your family group.

Familylab

Why? To analyze those family transactions which usually cause uncomfortable feelings if not an outright quarrel; to practice some ways of interaction that may be new for your family.

When/Where? The first and second of these exercises may be done in the context of a family discussion. Both will require at least an hour of uninterrupted, comfortable time when all participants are relaxed and alert. Although there are many Transactional Analysis materials available today, most of these activities were designed for adults and older (teen-aged) children. As you become familiar with the concepts, you may explain them to your younger children, and then perhaps do the exercises with them. The third exercise is one of a number of variations that can be done for fun, during a meal or while you are traveling.

How? 1. Explain the various types of transactions described in the text, so that all participants are speaking the same language. Then, together diagram some recent family transactions. What "tape" was playing in the head of each participant at the time of the exchange? Remember that the three states have nothing to do with chronological age. Your six or seven-year-old may occasionally bring you up short when she listens to your Child's outburst, then replies with her Adult, for example.

Next, pretend that you could do the transactions over again. This time, how would you play the roles? In other words, redesign the transactions as you would like them to go. How do the different lines sound as you say them? Would it be possible or worth it for you to learn to respond to similar transactions in this new way?

2. A sociogram is a diagram of the relationships between the various participants in a particular discussion or decision process. The occasion may be a mealtime segment, or it may be the selection of a television program. The arrows in the following sociogram indicate the person speaking in each transaction, and the person spoken to.

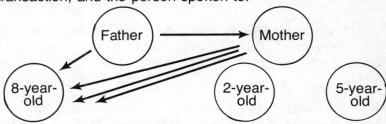

In this diagram, it is obvious that the mother is doing most of the talking, and the focus of her conversation is one child. Neither of the other two children is involved. The eight-year-old says nothing either.

Such a diagram shows the focus of a conversation, as well as the amount of interaction. Are there people who are left on the fringe of the interchange? Is one person doing all of the talking? Or does everyone do some talking? Are there people who are spoken to but who do not respond?

Ordinarily, one person serves as a secretary for each transaction. That person fills in the diagram for five minutes or so, then the conversation stops while the participants discuss the picture that resulted. Or you may tape record a discussion, then everyone can help to draw the sociogram as you listen to the recording. That has the advantage of allowing everyone to be included in the conversation you are analyzing.

How is your sociogram typical of most of your family transactions? Would your sociogram fit many other family discussions, or would they be different? How? If you could re-design the conversation, how would you do it? Rehearse the new way, roleplaying the various parts until they look like what you want. How do you feel about the new way? Would it be worthwhile to bring the new pattern into more of your ordinary conversation?

3. If your family were portrayed in the Sunday comic section, which cartoon strip would it resemble most? For example, my mother saw herself as Louisy Smith. Most of us recognize ourselves in one of the "Peanuts" characters. In what ways are you like the character you chose? Are your family conversations like those of the cartoon strip you chose? In what ways? What does your selection say about your family?

Chapter 2

Listening

Mrs. Webb: Emily, come and help me string these beans for the winter. George Gibbs let himself have a real conversation, didn't he? Why, he's growing up. How old would George be?

Emily: I don't know.

Mrs. Webb: Let's see. He must be almost sixteen. . .

Emily: Mama, will you answer me a question, serious?

Mrs. Webb: Seriously, dear—not serious.

Emily: Seriously,—will you?

Mrs. Webb: Of course, I will.

Emily: Mama, am I good looking?

Mrs. Webb: Yes, of course you are. All my children have got good features; I'd be ashamed if they hadn't.

Emily: Oh, Mama, that's not what I mean. What I mean is: am I *pretty*?

Mrs. Webb: I've already told you, yes. Now that's enough of that. You have a nice young pretty face. I never heard of such foolishness.

Emily: Oh, Mama, you never tell us the truth about anything.

Mrs. Webb: I *am* telling you the truth.

Emily: Mama, were *you* pretty?

Mrs. Webb: Yes, I was, if I do say it. I was the

> prettiest girl in town next to Mamie Cartwright.
>
> Emily: But, Mama, you've got to say *something* about me. Am I pretty enough ... to get anybody ... to get people interested in me?
>
> Mrs. Webb: Emily, you make me tired. Now stop it. You're pretty enough for all normal purposes. Come along now and bring that bowl with you.
>
> Emily: Oh, Mama, you're no help at all.[1]

1. Do you sometimes wish you knew more about the members of your family?

2. What is your reaction when someone listens to you attentively and sensitively?

3. Are you a good listener?

If people in the helping professions can be said to have a "guru," it is probably Carl Rogers. Consequently, one would expect him to have originated a complicated technique or designed an intricate formula. On reading his books or watching films of his clients, however, it becomes apparent that Rogers uses the simplest approach imaginable. He **listens.**

And what happens when he listens? People who come to him with vague but troubling fears discover for themselves what those fears are—and then the solution is within reach. People who are immobilized by their problems discover within themselves the power and strength to take command of them.

In listening, Rogers found his own life enriched. For example, in *Becoming Partners,* he listens as representatives of a variety of non-traditional marriage forms discuss

---

[1] Thornton Wilder, "Our Town", from *Three Plays by Thornton Wilder* (New York: Harper and Row, Publishers), 1957.

their way of life with him. He finds for himself a deeper appreciation of the form that he has chosen, and a greater awareness of the contributions that his wife and children have made to it.

In a relationship where the participants have learned to listen sensitively, both speaker and hearer grow. Usually, however, the issue is not so much a conviction about the value of listening as it is a frustration about **how** to do it. Parents of teenagers, especially, will relate their frustrations with conversations that proceed like this:

"School is dumb and I hate it!"

"What happened today?"

(Slammed bedroom door)

or "Girls sure can be stupid."

"Did something happen between you and Carol?"

"Naw."

Following Carl Rogers' emphasis on the importance of listening as helping, other psychologists have developed techniques and formulas to aid us in understanding listening as a skill. Parent Effectiveness Training (PET) teaches listening as a formula that can be acquired and adjusted to one's own style. In dealing with listening, PET assumes that we all sometimes say one thing when we mean another. We use a code to speak about matters that are not clear in our own minds, or about those which we feel are risky to share. Thus, a child who is a "big girl now" but who nevertheless is apprehensive about the first day at school or the first (or second) visit to the dentist will probably be afraid or embarrassed to say, "I am really anxious about this undertaking, and know that you will understand if I cry a bit right now." What you will probably hear is something like, "Mommy, my tummy hurts this morning."

Because as parents, we are usually busy and nearly always intent on finding immediate solutions, our reply may be either, "Big girls aren't afraid" or, "Let me take your temperature." Neither approach touches the problem. Instead, it would be more helpful to look at the feelings this daughter might be allowing us to glimpse in the hope that we will understand.

So we begin with a guess. It **is** the first day of school, and although she was excited when we went to choose her school outfits, she has been quiet about the subject lately. She looks more subdued than sick. So I check out with her what I think she may be saying: "You're worried about beginning school today?"

Several possibilities may follow. If she really is frightened about school, I have named her fear. That means that I know what fear is; she is not alone in this experience, nor is she bad or odd or disappointing to me. That realization is itself a great relief. My response also means that I am sincerely interested in knowing more about her feelings; otherwise, I would have opted for one of the standard, immediate solutions. Nothing is worse than a story that isn't heard, but she knows that I am able to listen, so she will probably accept my invitation and talk about the problem. If her stomachache had this for its cause, it will go away. And ultimately she may decide that she is strong and powerful enough to risk the first day of school. Perhaps she and I can do something together that will help to make the experience less formidable. Whatever the specific results of our conversation, I will certainly know more about the situation than I did from her initial declaration.

Although this sensitivity is probably often our intention in our dealings with members of our family, it is usually not the pattern of response that we are accustomed to giving. We may be used to equating the giving of help with supplying solutions rather than with listening, which is usually seen as a passive response. Sometimes we moralize, or tell about our own experiences in the hope that the child's faith in **our** success will give support. To test the effectiveness of these approaches, however, try to remember your own childhood reaction to sentences that began with, "When I was your age . . ." or, "You know, the Bible says . . ." My sister and I were still small, alone, and quite far from home when she caught her finger in a car door. A passing elderly stranger gave her a Bandaid and said soothingly, "There, there. I always told **my** girls, 'It'll heal before you get married.' " That aphorism was little consolation to her.

The difficulty with giving solutions at the beginning of a

conversation is that, as in the case of the fearful first grader, the situation as it is first stated is seldom the real cause of the upset. Once the person has had a chance to talk the problem out, the solution becomes apparent, and it is often something that the other can do unaided. Giving solutions too easily is akin in its effect to making light of the problem or resorting to sarcasm. These responses imply that the person has either overstated the difficulty or is incapable of coping with it.

So the key to listening sensitively is to be alert to feelings as they are expressed by words and gestures. Once you think that you know what the feeling is, check your intuition out with the sender of the message. There is nothing lost if your guess is incorrect; your attempt shows your concern. And it is an invitation to the sender to try again. Emily's trepidation concerns her popularity, not the issue of whether she has come from handsome stock. The nostalgia that the theatrical moment invokes in us is based on our recognition of those lines when they have been said in **our** families. But the moment might have been one of greater closeness between parent and child had Emily's mother helped her to talk about her mingled joy and timidity in the face of George's attentions. Then, her response might have been, "I think so, but you sound as though you're worried about it."

It must be admitted that this sort of listening does require concentration. Unfortunately, problems often come up during the 10 minutes preceding dinner. Yes, in families, the need for listening doesn't always come at opportune times. The harsh responses that cut off communication are usually resorted to out of desperation. Rather than that, however, explore some ways of letting the other person know that you are concerned and wish to be helpful but that your own needs at the minute are so pressing that you can't give the attention you would like to be able to give. I tried arranging my schedule for supper preparation so that I was less pressed when listening needed to be done. I don't think that our household suffered from the weekday substitution of casseroles for dishes which required closer attention. Also, simply stating the dilemma is helpful. Then agree on a better time for discussion. Otherwise, those who come to you may feel that you are turning them off. If they don't realize your concerns, they assume that you aren't interested. They may react with anger or sadness, neither being conducive to clear communication.

Familylab

Why? To become more aware of the value and technique of careful listening.

When/Where? These exercises may be done alone, by you and your spouse, or with older children. Allow 30 minutes for an orientation to the project, regular times (daily or so) for checkups, and at least 30 minutes to an hour for the final processing.

How? 1. Discuss together what qualities you like to find in a listener. Compile a list. Talk about why being listened to is enjoyable and helpful.

2. Sometime during the week, choose a listening situation in which you pretend that you can't talk back to the other person. Instead, use every non-verbal way of communicating your interest that you can think of. Watch what happens. If you seldom do this, be prepared for some incredulity, perhaps even some mistrust from your speaker-partner.

3. Another time, try to reflect only the feelings you hear back to the speaker: "You mean that you are worried about . . ." or "You sound excited about . . ." Again, what happens?

4. Agree to be sensitive this week to the quality of listening in your home. Try to make sure that you have an opportunity for thoughtful exchange with every other member of your household by the end of the week.

5. When you get together for your follow-up, compare notes of this project. Did you learn anything about each other? Did anyone's behavior change? In what ways? How did it feel to be listened to? To really hear someone else? Do you feel differently toward anyone you've listened to?

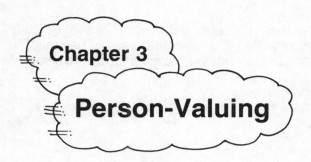

Chapter 3

Person-Valuing

The other morning, our Sunday morning radio minister told this story on his program. A family came into a restaurant for lunch. The waitress took the orders of the family members one by one until she came to the youngest, a little boy of about six or seven. "And what would you like?" the waitress

asked. "*I'll* order for him," the mother interrupted. "What would *you* like?" the waitress repeated, undaunted, to the child. "I'd like a hamburger," the little boy whispered shyly. "What would you like on your hamburger?" continued the waitress. "I'd like catsup and pickles," he replied. "And onions and tomato?" inquired the waitress. "Wow, yes," he declared. The waitress moved to the order window, and placed the orders, concluding with a flourish, "And a hamburger... with THE WORKS!" The small boy turned to his mother. "Listen, Mommy. She thinks I'm real!" he exalted.

18

1. Have you ever fantasized leaving your family, feeling that they wouldn't notice your absence until the dishes needed doing or the lawn needed mowing?

2. Have you ever secretly wished that your marriage were a little more like the Geritol television commercial: "This is my wife and I love her. . ."

3. Do you worry about any of your children because they have low self-images?

4. Do family members sometimes seem moody and easily depressed?

When the topic is insecurity, lack of self-confidence, and feeling of little personal worth, the person who comes to mind is Charlie Brown. "I think I can understand your fear of libraries, Linus," he says one day. " 'Library fever' is similar to other mental disturbances. You fear the library rooms because they are strange to you. You are out of place. All of us have certain areas in which we feel out of place." "Oh? In what area do you feel out of place, Charlie Brown," replies Linus. "Earth!" cries Charlie.[1]

There used to be a time when all illnesses were said to be based on an imbalance of one of the four fluids that were thought to control the body. In speaking of personality problems, we can often trace the cause—with considerably more accuracy than early physicians traced physical problems—to a lack of self-worth. Most of us don't value ourselves, and we are thus constantly on the watch for ways of dealing with and compensating for this.

Our society doesn't help, either. Here, our worth is equated with our productiveness; our value is seen in terms of money. For example, women become defensive when they define themselves as "homemakers" or "housewives." They aren't paid for that, and so they feel less valuable than the neighbor

---

[1]Robert L. Short. *The Gospel According to Peanuts.* (Richmond, Virginia: John Knox Press) 1964. p. 78.

who is employed outside the home. Conversely, men often see themselves as wage earners and equate this with personal value. Families in which the father is out of work or is unable to hold a job for any of a variety of legitimate reasons are often under great strain. This is not solely because money is tight, but primarily because the father's role is identified with earning the living for the rest of the family. When this is no longer possible within the traditional definitions of our society, the father feels that his value, perhaps even his right to live, is called into question.

A relationship in which one or both of the members feel valueless is inevitably strained. "I never felt that women should be assertive," said one wife. "I didn't finish college and I didn't think that I was smart enough to be able to hold a job. I really didn't feel that I was worthwhile as a person so I needed my husband to tell me that I was all right and when he forgot to do this, I got angry at him. After all, it wasn't just a matter of forgetfulness; he was neglecting to affirm my existence."

One problem is that this places too much responsibility on the shoulders of the other. A second problem is that if a person has the power of affirmation, this also implies the power of destruction. Thus, it is absolutely necessary to the relationship that one be constantly affirmed, supported, and praised. But the recipient can't really accept the praise, and so resorts to all sorts of gymnastics to deal with it. The message is, "You can make me feel valuable and worthwhile, but you're also a reminder that I've chosen not to do that for myself. Damn!"

Ultimately, the one who is constantly called upon to validate the other feels manipulated, as though his/her only contribution to the relationship is to shore up the other. It's a vicious circle.

The importance of this notion is evidenced by the great number and variety of images that are used by contemporary writers. Virginia Satir speaks of an old iron kettle that was used in her family to store a wide variety of commodities. Thus, self-esteem is spoken of in terms of feeling full, empty, dirty or cracked. Claude Steiner tells the tale of the "Warm

Fuzzies" which people at one time gave freely to each other. Self-esteem and the willingness and ability to esteem others go hand-in-hand, according to the image.

Eric Berne speaks of games as methods that people use to avoid intimacy. "If people really knew me, they would see that I'm evil, worthless, incapable, unloved, etc." goes the rationale. The second chorus is, "If I admit that I really am good, valuable, capable and loved, I would have to take responsibility for myself—and SUCCEED!"

Dr. Thomas Harris uses the terms, "I'm OK—You're OK." He breaks with others in Transactional Analysis in claiming that children begin by feeling NOT OK. In their eyes, everyone else is OK. But as parental strokes and rewards are less automatic—the child becomes too old for babying—the child adopts an "I'm not OK—You're not OK" stance. When the youngster is able to gain satisfaction and power, the position changes to "I'm OK—You're not OK."

At one point in her show, "Appearing Nitely," Lily Tomlin suddenly collapses in the center of the stage. After several moments of silence, she speaks from her position on the stage floor: "I notice that none of you got up to see what happened. Remember, we're all in this alone." And in a very real sense we are. We cannot give others self-esteem, we cannot make them feel OK, we cannot force them to give up gameplaying.

But we can help. If it is so common for people to feel "Not OK," what enables them to break out of that pattern? First, people change when feeling NOT OK hurts too much. "I really don't know whether I'm smart enough to join you," says the whine of the NOT OK housewife when her neighbors invite her to an enrichment course at the YWCA. "Fine, then we'll meet you again sometime," they respond over their shoulders. "Dear, what would I do without you to take care of me and protect me," coos the dependent "clinging vine" wife to her husband. "I don't need another child; I want an adult partner," he says on his way out the door.

People change if they become bored with the shelters they've built for themselves. "I'm 35," mourned a friend of mine, "and I feel stuck." George Gray, one of the characters

Edgar Lee Masters created for his *Spoon River Anthology,* speaks of the ship at harbor pictured on his gravestone. "In truth it pictures not my destination/But my life."[1] Some never become bored enough.

Finally, people change when they discover that they can. It may be a project that succeeds, an opinion that is listened to, an experience of the exhilaration that accompanies honest assertiveness.

How, then, do we help our children feel "full pot," "OK," satisfied to overflowing with "Warm Fuzzies"? First, we avoid discounting them. When we expose their feelings to humiliation, when we try to persuade them that they aren't really feeling the way they think they are, when we subject them to inflexible rules, we are helping them to feel worthless. "Nonsense, you're too old to be afraid of the dark," "Haven't I told you a million times?" and "Why can't you be like your brothers and sisters?" all chip away at the child's sense of self-esteem.

We help our children to feel strong and worthwhile when we allow them to make their own decisions, and correspondingly, when we let them deal with the ramifications of those decisions. Children are capable of various types of decisions generally much earlier than we are willing to believe. One mother told of giving her nine-year-old son the responsibility for doing his own laundry—when she became tired of finding his dirty clothes on the closet floor when the laundry was already done. Although this had all of the earmarks of a punishment, he was thrilled. He and his friend made a weekly pilgrimage to the laundromat, where they enjoyed TV in addition to the glorious autonomy of handling their own money and neatly folding their own clothes the way they wanted them.

Occasionally, children make mistakes. They do not need us to remind them; they already know what they are. But they do need us to help them develop a sense of community—"I'm OK—You're OK." Children's awareness of the rights of others and attention to their own rights go hand in hand. Our

---

[1] Paul Molloy ed. *Poetry USA.* (New York: Scholastic Book Svcs)1968. p.24.

laundry   toys
tools
shoes
dishes

children should know that we need some time for ourselves, for example, and they should know when they have infringed upon our legitimate rights.

With this attention to the rights of all in community comes the corresponding benefit of belonging to a group whose members care for and value each other. Assertiveness and growth are awkward; the role of the community is to support its members in the learning process. "He's so ugly that only his mother could love him," goes the old joke. The truth is that occasionally we are all so ugly that only those who love us and support us could tolerate us. The family should be that type of community.

The Tomlin program begins with a tiny child's voice that chants from the wings, "I'm not afraid of anything." Now **that's** a child with a strong self-image. The family is the arena with the most potential—and a vitally important role to play—in the development of a sense of personal value. It **is** scary to be important and strong and worthwhile enough to be oneself.

Familylab

Why? To consider as a family the unique contribution made by each member and to explore and experience the regard that members have for each other. To take responsibility for developing strengths you would like to have.

When/Where? Note that this is not time for Puritanical self-depreciation or inferiority complexes but for willingness to be open about your positive attributes. If you do this yourself, allow at least an hour. If you do this as a family, you will need more time, and you may even find it helpful to do the process in several sessions or to work with one person taking a turn at each session.

How:

1. With younger children, one person can serve as secretary, listing items for the other applicants. With older children, all keep their own lists. First, think of all the things you do well, all the things you are proud of having done, all the things that contribute to your feelings of accomplishment. List these positive accomplishments, your successes of the past. Be specific.

2. Now select someone you know to be sensitive to others, someone who listens well. Or do this step with the entire family. Examine together the successes you have listed, so that you can identify the strengths that were utilized to achieve them. For example, if you are proud of being a good babysitter, the qualities involved might be responsibility, honesty, ingenuity. If you keep your room clean, that involves generosity, helpfulness, and perhaps obedience. If you are good at your job, that may mean that your strengths are patience, a head for numbers, an artistic sense, skill in managing people, etc.

3. You now have two lists—a list of accomplishments and a list of personal strengths. Yes, this is really you. Now ask your partner or the other members of the family if they know of or have observed any other qualities that you have not listed, skills you may have overlooked or undervalued. Be sure your helpers give specific examples so that you can get a handle on the skill, talent or strength. For example, it probably won't be helpful to say, "You have a nice personality." "You help me when I ask, without complaining," however, is clear.

4. Ask the other person or family members to help you analyze what might be keeping you from utilizing all your strengths. Explore together ways in which you can free yourself from factors which limit the utilization of your strengths. List these as barriers to full realization of your potential. For example, "My impatience means that I don't finish work that could bring me great satisfaction."

5. Now you have a list of your past achievements and successes, a list of your present skills and personal

strengths, and a list of barriers keeping you from using those strengths to fullest advantage. Next, set a goal for improving either the quality of your strengths or the number of them. Plan only for one week in the beginning.

My goal is:

My strengths are:

The ways in which I will use my strengths to accomplish the goal are:

I will know that my goal is accomplished when. . .

For example, your goal may be to persevere longer at tasks which you find difficult. Your strength in a related area may be your skill with your hands, as in craft work. Thus, during the coming week, you may finish a project that you once began but never finished.

6. Plan a family meeting at the end of the week at which all of you review your plans. Do any goals need revision? Were there any new realizations or experiences? How does each person feel about the exercise?

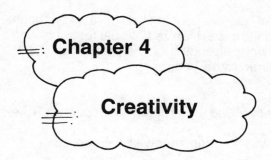

Chapter 4

Creativity

The occasion was several months into the school year, and Lynn was delighted with kindergarten. She was a lively child, full of plans and ideas, so everyone was relieved when she seemed to be enjoying school so much. Disillusionment hit when the class made Christmas cards for the children's parents. The teacher explained the project, then instructed the students to come up to her desk, one by one, and take a sheet of construction paper for a card. She went on with other matters, and by the time she rotated among the desks to Lynn's place, Lynn had two cards in progress.

In a rage, the teacher chastised her for disobeying orders, and tore one of the cards into tiny pieces which she put in the trash. Lynn held her tears until she reached her own home that afternoon, but then they flowed in earnest. In the first place, her mother related after unravelling the story, Lynn could not conceive of making one card for *both* parents. After all, she reasoned, one birthday—one card. Why not the same on this occasion? Second, she could not understand why the second card had been destroyed. If a shortage of paper meant that each child could have only one piece, the restriction made sense. She could admit that she was wrong, and would apologize. But even then, once the paper was marked, it could not be used by another child—so why tear it up?

*1. Do you ever find yourself wondering how **your** mother survived three rainy days in a row?*

2. What outlets do you have for your creative energy?

3. How does one foster creativity?

4. Do you ever feel like tap dancing, whether you know how or not?

5. What do you do when you wish there were a different way of doing something?

Human nature, schools, and society being what they are, this won't be the last time that Lynn will encounter this kind of problem. In the trend toward humanistic education of the 60's and 70's, educators talked a great deal about creativity and ways of encouraging students to develop their feelings and senses. In fact, however, simply because of the regimentation that rules the huge schools of today, that may be the most unlikely place for true creativity to emerge. Lynn's teacher undoubtedly saw no connection between the fostering of Lynn's creativity and her reaction to her behavior. Nevertheless, if Lynn is not to lose her imaginativeness and originality, she will need support from other quarters.

Thus, the current pressure to "return" to the basic skills of reading and mathematics in school curricula should not signal an end to the developing of creativity. The fear that it will do so is based on the false premise that creativity is a children's activity. While adult creativity undoubtedly is often based on childhood openness to exploration, creativity is a source of joy and fulfillment for adults as well as children.

Creativity is not simply a matter of being able to draw, sculpt or embroider. Those are art forms. Art is a system of communication, a means of expression. Creativity is more. It is rooted in the ability to see things in a new light, to be able to imagine a different way. We all have the opportunity to be creative when we are dissatisfied with something. For example, our present ability to fly from one place to another is built on the age-old human dissatisfaction with earthbound locomotion. "Why do we have to do it **this** way? is the question at the base of many of the appliances that make our lives more comfortable. And already, people look at **them**, ask why, and develop ways of living without them.

"What if . . .?" and "Why?" and "Why not?" are questions that call creativity into action. It is tragic when people become so used to things as they are or so dependent on social approval that they no longer can or will ask those questions.

So creativity is not a child issue. It can be a source of immense satisfaction for adults as well. However, there **are** things which parents can do to call forth the native creativity of their children. First, parents can model creativity. Usually, they find themselves in the role of defender of the status quo. "Why do we do things this way?" children ask, and the habitual parental responses are, "Because **I** said so," "Because it's done this way," "Because this is the way everybody else does it," or "Because I don't have time to argue." Much of this is necessitated by the parental role as interpreter of social custom. But much isn't, and children are freed to look for alternatives when they see that their parents also occasionally ask the same question.

In fact, children usually rejoice in the creativity of their parents. The fellow across the street, tired of hot summer afternoons and/or high air conditioning costs, tinkered with a collection of odds and ends, and now his family relaxes in the coolness of an automatic ventilation system that looks as though it could suck a body right out through the roof. His children bring relative strangers in from the street to witness to the skill of a father who refused to limit his alternatives.

We can foster the imagination of our children by occasionally creating with them. Play, the essence of creativity, is not something that children do and parents interrupt when it's time for supper. It **is** something that gains additional value and status in the estimation of children when their parents also engage in it. Each early summer, Columbus, Ohio, sponsors an arts festival on the sprawling lawns of the statehouse. A regular feature of the week is a mountain of scrap lumber—small blocks and strips—and quart contain- ers of wood glue. Parents can leave their children there, or they may join them. Any hour of the day, it is possible to find the entire range of attitudes toward creativity in action at that area. At one point, there were some children who were thoroughly happy by themselves in corners, gluing and rearranging wood to their hearts' content. Others worked on joint projects. Some youngsters were intent on creating useful objects—a shelf or bookends, for example. Others worked on shapes that would be recognizeable images. One was building a truck, another a toy train, etc. Still others were completely thrilled with wood pieces glued together simply because they looked like what they wanted—an abstract, we would say.

In the center of the lawn was one father who brought his five-year-old over to the stack of wood. "Now, you sit still and keep out of trouble," he warned, "while I show you how to do this," In contrast, there were whole families working on individual or group projects; children and adults held equal rights in the work, and all were enjoying the process.

Children need to know our acceptance of their efforts and our occasional (at least) willingness to play, too. They probably don't need our specific instructions on **how** as often as we are inclined to give them, however.

We all have had the uncomfortable experience of telling a youngster that we think a school art project is very good, only to be told that the child thinks it's "dumb." It is seldom helpful to give an evaluation of another's projects. Frankly, how good are some of the scribbles that decorate our refrigerator doors? The artistic skill in evidence is not relevant. What **is** relevant is our feelings about it. "I really like this," is more supportive than, "Michelangelo would be green with envy," or any insinuation to that effect.

It is also most helpful to encourage children to talk about their feelings for their work. "You're really pleased with this," is a response that enables the child to reflect on the joy of creating and the frustration that creativity necessarily in- volves. In the same vein, "What is it supposed to be," will get you in trouble, especially if the piece isn't supposed to be anything other than a dabbling with color or line. "Tell me about it," allows the child to relive the creating experience again. It's much like the pleasure that we take in telling a good story. It's really a letdown when our "Did you ever hear about the . . .?" meets an immediate "Yes, I did,"

Finally, toy companies in the past few years have responded to the consumers' interest in playthings that are supposed to appeal to children's love of free play and abstract art. But clay and wood scraps don't sell as well as more involved, structured kits, and so there are on the market all manner of clay moulds and kits. Nevertheless, children persist in their delight with cheap, unbreakable, formless toys like sandpiles and large cardboard boxes. Tightly structuring creativity is less helpful than fostering experimentation with pure form, color, shape and texture. And it's usually cheaper, too.

The human ability to create is really the Child in action. In TA terms, our Parent imposes rules and structures. The Child delights in imagining alternatives and playing with a multitude of possibilities. The Child doesn't mind getting dirty, and it doesn't matter to the Child if an invention actually lacks the convenience or efficiency of a conventional form. It's different, and that's the fun of it. This Child is guileless, and indulges in creative experimentation simply for the pleasure of it. This Familylab proposes some activities for exploring the concept of creativity as a family unit.

Familylab

Why? To explore together some avenues for developing the creativity of the family members.

When/Where? The following activities are designed to be done at a variety of times and places, ranging from an evening or weekend afternoon together to a few minutes at the table. Writing activities can be done with younger children if someone acts as a secretary for them. Or use a cassette tape recorder, to capitalize on their excitement at hearing their own voices. Some of these suggestions make good activities for travel hours.

How? 1. Poetry: Children have an innate feeling for the "right" words for things; before they are socially conditioned, they often may be more accurate than adults. Second, there is something about words that makes them great playthings. However, we soon become so indoctrinated with the serious business of using the English language that we lose the fun of it, and half of the value of words is gone. The following exercises are word games that can be played anywhere, and the results are poems in the sense that poetry is words used in an unusual way.

a) Compile a list of quiet words, noisy words, slow words, quick words. These words may **sound** quiet, or may actually mean quiet.

b) Write a line to suggest:
   An express train
   A rider on a horse
   A child asleep
   Wind in the trees
   A hunting dog running
Try moving your hands, arms and shoulders in time to the line you have written.

c) Make a list of words as follows:
   Words that describe pleasing smells
   Words that describe harsh sounds
   Words that describe sharp edges
   Words that describe shiny objects

d) Make a list of "sound words" arranged in order of intensity, dealing with:
   Explosives (beginning with "pop")
   Animal noises (beginning with "squeak")
   Traffic (begin with "hum")

e) Compose specific vivid phases to replace the following general, colorless phrases:
An expensive automobile
A dark night
A terrifying sight with an alarming sound
A sickening taste with an unpleasant smell

f) Describe as precisely as you can:
The sound of a typewriter
The feel of a dog's nose
The smell of an old attic
The taste of crackers
The sensation in your stomach as you ride an escalator

g) Try composing couplets after these models:
Did you ever see a snake?
Darting, fork-tongued, wide-mouthed.

An acrobat hanging from a tightrope;
A yo-yo dangling from its string.
In the first model, a "Did you ever see a _____?" question is followed by several tightly packed adjectives. In the second example, one subject is paired with another which matches it visually. Another example:
A full moon in a dark sky;
A white button on a black dress.

h) Combine your poetry writing talents with your artistic abilities. On a sheet of drawing paper write a word in the shape that the word denotes. Thus, **tall** is drawn with long thin lines, **tree** would be written in the shape of a trunk surrounded with small red apples, etc. This is great fun and calls forth imagination. The possibilities are endless, and it is another way of becoming sensitive to the various ways that words can operate.

i) Become word-list-keepers. Keep lists of "sound" words, of words that denote visual appeal, of words that name unpleasant feelings, etc.

2. Dance: As with so many other artistic expressions, children move naturally and gracefully when they are young, and only later learn to be self-conscious. Then we lose our natural self-expressiveness. Freedom to move as you feel is something that adults can model for their children, and so these exercises could well be done by the whole family. (And if this isn't too much to add to the chaotic pre-supper operations, try to move into the livingroom or family room for a danced supper grace before meals.

a) If you already did the poetry exercises, take some of your poems, stand apart from each other, read the poem, and (with closed eyes) move like the feeling or mood expressed in the poem. Afterwards, reflect momentarily on the feelings you had during the experience.

b) Find a clear spot, curl up, close your eyes, and climb into your favorite bad feeling—depression, oppression, sadness, etc. Move around to match the feeling. What do you really want to do with that feeling? Act that response out.

c) Again, find a clear place in your home. Then curl up in a ball and listen to your favorite instrumental recording. Let the muscles and sinews of your body move as they will in response to the rhythm of the music. While you do this have your eyes closed and visually imagine a scene to accompany the feeling you have when you hear this recording.

Slowly allow yourself to stand up, remembering to sit before you stand. Gracefully let your body sway to the rhythm of the music. Free your arms and legs to respond in whatever way seems natural as you listen to the music. Clap for yourself when your dance is ended.

d) As in previous number b above, take a favorite happy emotion and following the same technique, act out the response in movement to the emotion or feeling.

3. Music: Creating music is easy. All you need is the desire to say something in a beautiful manner, and that something must mean a great deal to you. It can be a way to share some very deep feelings you may not be able to put into words.

a) Select something from your treasury of experience and emotion that you would like to share with others.

b) Take a musical instrument, whether you know how to play it or not, and begin playing around with it until you develop a short pattern that sounds like whatever you are feeling and want to share with another.

c) If you cannot write or read music, then a tape recorder is good for helping you to remember the finished theme when you have composed it.

d) Next have some fun with your theme. Sing it or play it backwards. Start on a different note and see what comes of your theme. Notice whether your theme falls naturally into any particular rhythm pattern. Fit another theme to be sung at the same time or played at the same time and see what happens to the harmony. Or do as many things as you can think of with your theme, keeping a record of all your research and discoveries.

e) Arrange your "Theme and Variations" for other people to play.

f) Gather some of your friends and form a trial concert where all those who play an instrument will do their thing with your theme. Expand this as far as you like. Include as many different instruments as you have available. Ask the musicians for suggestions for arranging the theme for a better sound. In the final analysis, however, you are the conductor with your theme.

4. Photography: Many people have cameras today and the speed with which our pictures are developed allows many interesting and exciting family projects.

a) Take the recording you have just made of "Theme and Variations" and arrange a set of slides to accompany the composition.

b) Using your favorite passage from Scripture or a special poem, arrange a set of your own pictures or slides to accompany the reading.

c) Select a favorite record (with or without words) and set up a group of slides to accompany the recording.

d) Save pictures of your family activities and then arrange them in a reading to be used during anniversary celebrations or for birthdays and other special family events.

e) Take the blank negatives that are sometimes returned to you and scratch off the black emulsion in designs or in words to be used in some of the photographic compositions. If you use color film that has been unexposed but developed, scratch lightly to reveal various levels of color that are visible when the slide is projected.

5. Although psychologists say that we use our dreams to problem-solve and to do all manner of emotional work, dreams are also where our creativity is unhampered by practicality or timidity. Many people say that they don't dream. What they are really saying is that they don't remember their dreams. We can remember them if we want to, especially if we are willing to practice a bit. Make a conscious resolution before retiring that you are going to remember at least one thing from your dreams. The next morning, try to recall at least one aspect of your dreams. If you do this as a family, talk about your intention at the supper table and share what you remember as you eat breakfast, even if for only a minute. Don't be discouraged if you don't remember anything the first time you try; sometimes it takes several days to get in the habit of remembering your dreams. Sharing dreams with other family members can be fun.

Suggested Reading

Bach, Dr. George, and Peter Wyden. *How To Fight Fair in Love and Marriage.* New York: William Morrow and Co., 1969.
The encyclopedia on fighting techniques for husbands and wives. Fighting may not be as invigorating a pastime as it sounds, but this book does deal with the pitfalls and techniques of marital uproars.

Berne, Eric, M.D. *Games' People Play.* New York: Grove Press, Inc., 1964.
Gives the foundation of Transactional Analysis, with descriptions of the many games people resort to in order to avoid intimacy.

Berne, Eric, M.D. *What Do You Say After You Say Hello?* New York: Grove Press, Inc., 1972.
The further development of the games theory into analysis of life scripts.

Brayer, Herbert O. and Zella W. Cleary. *Valuing in the Family.* San Diego: Pennant Press, 1973.
Structured family workshop approach to various virtues and personality traits.

Briggs, Dorothy C. *Your Child's Self-Esteem.* New York: Doubleday, 1970.
Enlarges on Parent Effectiveness Training concepts, centering on the importance of the child's sense of self worth.

Dodson, Dr. Fitzhugh. *How To Parent.* New York: New American Library, 1970.
Good description of the various stages of child development, with an exhaustive bibliography of books and records for children as well as parents.

Dodson, Dr. Fitzhugh. *How To Father.* New York: New American Library, 1974.
An updated version of How To Parent, this time directed at fathers.

Ginott, Dr. Haim. *Between Parent and Child.* New York: Macmillan Publishing Company, 1965.

Common sense and highly readable approach to family relationships.

Ginott, Dr. Haim. *Between Parent and Teenager.* New York: The Macmillan Co., 1969.
Sympathetic understanding of adolescents and parents' struggles with them; common sense advice about listening, dealing with rebellion, values, rules and other issues.

Gordon, Dr. Thomas. *Parent Effectiveness Training.* New York: Peter H. Wyden, Inc., 1970.
Patterns for helpful listening, expression of feelings, and no-lose problem solving.

Gordon, Dr. Thomas. *P.E.T. In Action.* New York: Wyden Books, 1976.
An expanded explanation of P.E.T. with illustrative case studies.

Gunther, Bernard. *Sense Relaxation.* New York: Collier Books, 1968.
A collection of exercises for individuals and couples to increase body awareness and decrease tension.

Gunther, Bernard. *What To Do Till The Messiah Comes.* New York: The Macmillan Co., 1971.
A companion volume to Sense Relaxation—both books are good for your own child.

Harris, Thomas A. *I'm OK–You're OK.* New York: Harper and Row, Publishers, 1967.
A popularization of Eric Berne's theory of games in human interaction; develops the notion of Parent, Child, and Adult, with applications to family living.

Homan, William E. *Child Sense: A Guide to Loving, Level-Headed Parenthood.* New York: Basic Books, Inc., 1977.
Chapters on love, discipline, independence, and problems with specific age groups. Incisive humor. You may not agree with his view that daycare centers are "inventions of the Devil," but you may skip that page (202) or think about his reasons for that judgment.

James, Muriel and Dorothy Jongeward. *Born To Win.* New York: Addison-Wesley Publishing Company, 1971.
A workbook approach to transactional analysis. Helpful in

making personal application of the Transactional Analysis concepts.

Jourard, Sidney N. *The Transparent Self.* New York: D. Van Norstrand, 1964.
Deals with the value of being one's real self with others, and the problems involved in concealing our thoughts and feelings.

Langley, Roger and Richard Levy. *Wifebeating: The Silent Crisis.* New York: E.P. Dutton, 1977.
Uses case studies to illustrate various situations in which wifebeating occurs, with startling but documented facts about the problem.

Lewis, Howard R. *Growth Games.* New York: Bantam Books, 1970
A catalogue of games to explore our own personality and our relationships. May be adapted to the family setting.

Missildine, Dr. W. Hugh. *Your Inner Child of the Past.* New York: Simon and Schuster, 1963.
Focuses on parenting oneself, and listening to the child in us, but also helps us to reflect on our present parenting patterns.

Neill, A.S. *Summerhill: A Radical Approach to Child Rearing.* New York: Hart Publishing Co., Inc., 1960.
Neill founded an English boarding school which operated under the philosophy that the school should fit the child. Sensitive approach to the needs of children.

Sax, Saville and Sandra Hollander. *Reality Games.* New York: Popular Library, 1972.
Another catalogue of games which families with older children may use to increase their awareness of each other and family operations and communication.

Sheehy, Gail. *Passages.* New York: E.P. Dutton and Co. Inc., 1974.
Through case studies, the author describes the stages of growth through which adults move. Helpful in understanding family relationships as they grow from adult needs.

Viorst, Judith. *It's Hard To Be Hip Over Thirty and Other Tragedies of Married Life.* Cleveland: New American Library, 1968.

Humorous, human approach to marriage and family living. You might try your hand at writing about your own experiences as she did.

Wahlroos, Sven. *Family Communication: A Guide To Emotional Health.* New York: Macmillan Publishing Co., Inc., 1974.

Emphasis on adult self-understanding in the context of the family. Tends to oversimplify, but fun to read anyway.

PART TWO

FAMILY ORGANIZATION

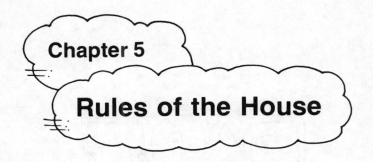

Chapter 5

Rules of the House

"Jennifer, now why are you crying? The baby pulled your hair? Well, honey, she didn't mean to do that. She's only a baby. You remember what we said about that. Don't throw your dolly on the ground; you know you aren't supposed to throw things. Pick

up your doll. Jennifer, come back here. Where are you going? Jennifer!! Come back here. Don't you dare turn your back when I'm talking to you. Where are you going? In the house? What do you want in the house? You aren't going in the house while I'm out here with the baby. You're not allowed to do that. Oh, all right. You can bring one toy—ONE toy—out here. No, you can't bring that out here; you know the rules about your Barbi doll clothes."

1. Do conversations beginning with lines such as "Mom, Mary is supposed to . . . and she isn't," ever take place at your house?

2. How about, "No, it isn't either my turn."

3. What principles govern the organization of your house?

4. What are the unspoken rules that everyone is supposed to know and obey?

5. How are the unspoken rules communicated?

In "Death of a Salesman," playwright Arthur Miller deals with the American Dream and the rules adopted by one family in order to support it. The cardinal rule is "Never lose!" Even more important to the family dynamic, however, is the rule which naturally follows: "Never admit it if you do lose."

On the surface, the family's failures are probably no greater than those encountered by most. Money never seems to stretch far enough and things wear out at about the time they are paid for. One son moves from job to job, seemingly rootless, while the other son looks only for a good time. At the age of 63, Willy Loman loses his job, along with his ability to deal with reality. But, in line with the family taboos, no one is allowed to talk about his suicide attempts. The mood of the play is oppressive with questions that could not be asked and pardons that were not allowed to be sought or given.

The function of rules is to maintain order. For the Lomans, order was identified with prosperity and reputation, and so the family rules were designed to protect those values. On the level of daily operation in the home, rules allow the family to circumvent the hassles that probably would accompany a separate allocation of tasks, for instance each time the dishes need doing. The family exists in greater peace when there are established rules for dealing with money, doing chores, punishing misconduct, allocating space, and providing for the rights of the individuals.

For example, when my friend and I host her nieces, aged four to 12, during summer vacations, one standing rule helps us to prevent wasted food when we go out to eat. Each child may order her own meal; the only qualification is that she must eat what she orders. Otherwise, the next time we go out, an adult orders for her. That way, we don't have to nag, and the youngsters understand the need for coordinating their appetites with their capacities.

Another function of rules is to provide a group with an identity, as well as with a sense of continuity with the past. "Because we've always done it this way," may be a valid reason for a particular rule. For instance, the Jewish people were identified by their adherence to the Law. It protected them from a variety of diseases and mishaps, and their observance of it set them apart from the other inhabitants of their world.

Similarly, one family related their experience with a family rule of reserving Sunday as "Family Day." There was usually a special family meal, and the members went places and did things with each other rather than with neighbors, friends, and business associates. "We found that we became an item of interest in the neighborhood," the parents related. "Our children were saying that they couldn't go to this and that activity because it was "Family Day," and pretty soon, the other kids were coming over to see what it was that we did together."

This function of rules tends to be a mixed blessing, however. Rules quickly solidify, and their origins become obscured. Then, rules become those things which we do even though no one is quite certain why. Anyone who has heard the old refrain, "But Dad (Mom), you let **him** do it!" can appreciate how quickly this happens. Individual circumstances are forgotten with time, and suggestions rapidly become canons, forming a Code of Family Law.

There is the old story about the wife who habitually cut hams in quarters before cooking. When her husband questioned the practice, her reply was that her mother had taught her that way. She was sure it was the "right" method, since her mother's cooking was unparalleled. Nevertheless, she did ask her mother the reason for this the next time they met. "Because in those days, I didn't have a pan large enough for a whole ham," was her reply.

Thus, despite the comfort and security provided by rules which have become a part of the family fabric, there is always the need to examine them and assess their value to the present, particular family unit. If one of the functions of family rules is to promote order, how much order in your family can be traced to the existence of rules? How is your life easier because there are established rules for doing things—and for who does them?

What is the source for rules in your family? Do they come from one parent or both? If they come from you as parents, where did you get them? Were they rules in the home in which you were reared? Did you get them from other parents who have shared their experiences with you? Were they superimposed? By whom? On whom?

How many of your family rules came into being through some process of discussion and mutual consent? Have many of your family rules arisen from situations which revealed a need? For example, duty assignments may have originated from the neglect of some jobs and popularity of others among the family members. Use of the family car may have been organized following a recognition of the needs of all family members.

Is your understanding of the reasons for existing family rules the same as that shared by other family members? For example, younger children may have an established and enforced time for going to bed. What is **their** understanding of the reason for this? Is it because you don't want them to be tired the following morning when you need them to be prompt risers? Is it because they get crabby when they don't get enough sleep? Is it because you need some time alone with your spouse? Is it because **you** are tired, and **you** get crabby when your children don't get enough sleep?

Sometimes we would like our children to follow our rules instantly, without question. But knowing the rationale behind a rule can't help but be an important factor no matter what the age of the child. "Because I said so," is an expression of our frustration more than an argument that impels intelligent compliance. "Because I need you to do this," is an acceptable reason for requiring a specific behavior. Saying **that** is more honest than conjuring motivations that sound less selfish and more altruistic.

For instance, "Children should be seen and not heard," sounds better than "I don't like it when you make a lot of noise when we have company." Nevertheless, there are many **adults** who are still obediently "seen and not heard." Sharing the rationale of family rules within the limits of the children's ability to understand (They are usually more perceptive and thoughtful than we think) insures that they will be flexible. They will be more capable of discarding rules as these become counterproductive, and more honest about setting their own rules as they feel that these are necessary.

Flexibility in the realm of rules is an emotional issue. It is a truism to say that we are most defensive about those rules whose value we are most unsure of. Since we do tend to identify them with our culture and its values, rules represent considerable security. Conversely, questioning society's formulas for behavior also brings it into question. For example, if I "let" my wife go against the rules of behavior for wives and mothers in our family tradition, what will be the outcome? Will our family maintain its identity? Will my leadership be called into question? Will my wishes be noted? WILL OUR CHILDREN GROW UP ALL RIGHT??

In thinking about our family rules, we cannot easily escape the question of how much order really is necessary. How many of those rules which operate in our family to maintain order could be dispensed with? If all of the members of the family were sensitive to each other's needs, would there need to be a calendar for the regimentation of dish washers and bed makers? If such awareness is lacking (as it is at some time in all families) is there any way of working on **that** instead of, or simultaneously with, working on a bigger and better house-duty calendar.

Obviously, there are some facets of living together that are mundane, a trial to the spirit of practically all community members. But dealing with as many of these as possible in terms of human consideration and thoughtfulness rather than resorting to a stated rule will help members to respond in a personal way to each other. Establishing rules to take discussion, initiative, and pleasant or unpleasant feedback out of the situation also removes an opportunity for intimacy.

So discussing family rules is a risk, especially if you intend to listen to the feedback which each member gives. What if your discussion reveals that all of your family rules are parent-imposed? In this day of talk about children's rights, that doesn't sound good—or does it? Your feelings on this issue will have a great deal to do with the type of material you discuss—and the way in which you discuss it.

What if you aren't consistent in the way in which you enforce rules? What if some of your family rules—and attitudes—need to be changed? Could you consider the possibility? Are you really in touch with these rules (spoken and unspoken) which actually are in operation in your family?

This Family lab offers a process for involving the entire family in an analysis of the rules in operation at your house. There is no answer so simple as saying that rules are bad, or that the ideal family is one which is completely governed by carefully defined formulas. This is your chance to see what your family rules look like and to make some decisions based on that picture.

Familylab

Why? To examine your family rules and the ways in which they were formulated and adopted so that forgotten rules can be renewed if this would serve a purpose, so that unstated rules can be brought to the surface and examined together, and finally so that the rationale behind existing rules can be clarified for all who are expected to obey them.

When/Where? You will need at least one hour for this activity, depending on the attention span of your children. Or the steps may be done in several sessions. Each session should be uninterrupted and without distraction of the TV in the background, etc.

How? 1. Imagine that you have decided to adopt a child about the same age as your own children. Together, you want to put down some directions for living in your family. Or if you and your spouse are doing this alone, imagine that you are describing your relationship for a handbook on survival at your house. You don't want new members to be uncomfortable or to get into trouble, so you need to be accurate about what is expected. One person is the secretary. Keep a list on a large sheet of paper so that everyone can see the items as they are mentioned.

List all of the rules in operation at your house. Some of them may not be observed uniformly, but if some member of the family expects them to be obeyed at least once in a while, put them on the list. For example, one rule at our house is that the utility building in the backyard should be kept locked. The reason is the protection from theft of the tools which we store there. Usually, however, we don't take our keys with us when we put the lawnmower away and so it sometimes isn't locked. But it should be. That's a house rule, even though it isn't regularly followed.

The point isn't to blame or praise family members for obeying or ignoring rules. Remember that you want to describe as accurately as possible all of the rules in operation. Some—perhaps most—may be complicated. Don't censor each other. If one person thinks that an item is a family rule, list it. For example, Susan says that Bill does the dishes on Saturday night. Bill thinks that he does the dishes on Saturday night only if he doesn't have a date that evening. Or it's all right to play with the baby during the sermon in church on Sunday, as long as you are Mom or Dad. If you are a child, you aren't allowed to wink at her so that she giggles. Cursing? That's all right if you are a parent or if you don't do it in public. Who are you allowed to disagree with in your family? How are you allowed to disagree? What are the rules for asking questions or voicing dissent?

2. If you are doing this process in two stages, you may wish to hang the paper in a prominant place such as the refrigerator door so that all members can think about the list and add rules to it if others come to mind before the next session. Or you may continue. Together, go over some of the questions in this unit. This will give you some idea of how rules come into being in your family.

3. How do you feel about the rules for your family and the way in which rules are made? Having looked at the whole picture, is there anything you would change? Are some of the rules outdated or clearly unfair? Are there trouble spots in your living together that might be smoothed out by additional or updated rules?

4. Once you have renovated the rules for your family, plan a follow-up meeting to be held in a week. At that time, discuss whether the changes or additions you have made are effective and helpful. Are there other rules that need similar renovations? Keep the list as a reference during the several weeks in which you are working on this topic. A periodic examination of household rules is helpful in preventing misunderstanding and unfairness, not to mention the difference in attitude when people have a role in the formulation of the rules by which they live.

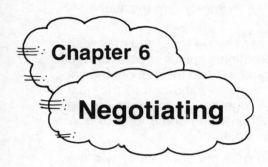

Chapter 6

Negotiating

Sharon: Last year, Jim and I decided that with three children and the rising cost of education, I would go back to work. I was excited about it. I mean, I had taught school until Judy was born, and I enjoyed my work

Jim: I thought she would like it, too. But lately, Sharon has been really difficult to live with. I get home from the office and she's in the kitchen tossing pans around. She jumps on the kids all during supper, and so we hurry through the meal so that the rest of us can "escape" to the TV set in the family room. But even after she is finished cleaning up the kitchen, she nags about the newspapers on the floor or the state of the kids' bedrooms.

Sharon: I feel bad about crabbing all the time. But I'm tired after my job, too. I come home, and although my working was something that we all agreed to undertake, I end up with the same household load that I had before.

Jim: Well, if you're asking me to help you in the kitchen, I won't do that. You don't like the way I do things there, and besides, the kitchen is too small. We'd fall over each other. Anyway, I'm not the only one you squawk at. Yesterday, I thought you would

> **never stop scolding Julie because she
> didn't hang up her clothes.**
> Sharon: **But surely she knew that I was tired. She
> and Sean refuse to keep their rooms clean.
> Eventually, I do it just because I can't
> stand the mess any longer . . . But I resent
> it.**

*1. In your family, do situations arise in which no one is
happy? In which everyone is upset with the status quo?*

*2. Do you have a process for dealing with these
times–short of sending everyone to a corner until the
bell rings?*

*3. Does your family have someone in charge of prob-
lem solving? How does that person feel about the
assignment?*

Recently, I conducted a workshop for parents at which the
topic was using techniques of negotiation in the family
setting. As I proceeded to explain the process, I sensed that if
there was no outspoken opposition, there was no particular
involvement either. I continued to the end of my presentation
when suddenly one participant exclaimed, "But that's exactly
what we do at work to deal with conflicts on our management
team!"

Then the questions began. All of them centered on the
relevance of a business technique for family problems. After
all, can children really participate in important family decisions? Blunt though this may sound, when parental needs
clash with children's needs, don't parental needs take
precedence? Isn't the process too involved for children?
Aren't kids pretty limited in their ability to think of solutions for
a problem? What happens when it doesn't work?

But it **does** work, I reiterated. I answered the questions and
responded to the objections, then asked the group to try the
technique during the following week. I guessed that most of
the trial situations would center on mealtime practices,
cleanliness of the children's rooms, television viewing or

another of the situations that usually are the occasion of family friction. I was right. The next week, the parents came with stories of some startling successes as well as some minor ones and a few false starts. All agreed, however, that the approach has possibilities. They were amazed at the sincerity and resourcefulness of their children, once they became involved. Also, they realized that their children's initial reluctance to try the process or refusal to take the process seriously was probably rooted in their previous experience of similar "Family Council" sessions that cloaked unilateral parental rules and demands. "Let's talk about it," often means "I'm going to tell you what I want you to do about your room (your table behavior, your bedtime, etc.)."

The successes were exciting. In one family, the youngest of four boys had reached the stage where he was crawling about the home. The mother was concerned that he would get one of the other boys' small toys and choke on it. When she presented her side of the problem, her sons initiated a plan to relegate that particular toy to a section of the garage, out of the baby's reach. She contrasted their willingness to comply with that suggestion with their consistent disregard of rules which she and her husband originated and enforced.

Another couple dealt with family transportation. The mother felt imposed upon by myriad chauffeuring trips for her children, and she especially resented their volunteering her services for school trips. The budget was strained in the "car expenses" column, but the eldest child, having recently become a duly licensed driver, felt that she deserved a chance at the family car. Through a negotiating process involving the entire family, everyone's problems and gripes were acknowledged. Then, when all were free to concentrate their energies on the issue, they discovered many ways of operating so that the needs of all were met. Previously, a parental suggestion that the children ride a bus or schedule their activities to avoid three trips to and from school in the same afternoon would have met with wails of desolation followed by "business as usual."

Other families dealt with mealtime chaos, by devising schedules that avoided conflict while allowing for the need to have a meal together. Parents with younger children worked on the perennial problem of balancing dietary likes and dislikes with kitchen logistics.

Whatever the situation, it is necessary that all members of the negotiating group be involved, that all are dissatisfied with the situation as it stands. For example, youngsters don't like carrots, but adults don't like ulcers. Teenagers don't like a lock on the refrigerator, but adults don't like to find tomorrow's lunch supplies gone! Kids feel invaded when Mom excavates their room, but mothers don't like to find Monday's dirty wash on the closet floor—on Tuesday. And Dads don't like to break a foot on scattered toys they encounter between the bedroom door and the goodnight kiss.

This initial assumption is vital. If only part of the family is unhappy with things as they are, if the problem belongs only to part of the group, compliance with any contract reached becomes a matter of a charitable contribution to the offended person's welfare. We may like to feel that people are generally altruistic, but over the long haul of family meals, schedules and cluttered bedrooms, altruism runs a bit thin. For negotiation to be appropriate and successful, everybody must stand to profit by the process.

Be sure to plan for a good time and place for the discussion. In the business world, problem solving is not done in the midst of the pressures that caused the conflict. Nor is it done at 5:50 on Friday afternoon. Agree on a time when all involved can devote an uninterrupted hour or so. Very small children will be able to go through an abbreviated process much more quickly, but older children will need enough time to do the procedure in greater detail.

First, define the issue, being sure to include all facets of the problem. Look at it from all angles, and once the whole picture is clear, write down your issue definition. Don't deviate from it during the discussion; you'll get bogged down. If other problems surface, reserve them for later sessions. Then brainstorm for possible solutions. Write down each suggestion as it is given, without any censoring or polishing. You'll probably have some funny suggestions; write them down, too. If you have a list of 40, the choice is better than if your list is limited to three or four. Besides, even the most outlandish suggestion may have possibilities or may be used as a springboard to an idea that would work.

When all the ideas have been listed, sift through them to find a plan that responds to all facets of the problem. Don't allow anyone to agree to the plan before they are completely satisfied. If you have brainstormed long enough, you will be able to find a solution that meets everyone's needs. Otherwise, dissatisfactions will eventually surface. For example, if Mom is so beguiled by everyone's concern over the messy room issue that she agrees to soften her demands, she'll soon be unhappy again.

Write down the plan you've agreed upon. Add to it complete details about job assignments, time deadlines, and dates for an assessment of the progress of the project. It is important that you be as specific as possible, although with younger children, you will need to work through the process before they reach the limits of their attention span. Make certain that each participant is happy with the arrangements, and make certain that all understand what they are agreeing to do. If you close as many loopholes as possible now, you'll avoid the frustrating choruses of "I didn't know you meant **that,**" later.

Finally, be sure to allow for renegotiating at the end of a trial period. In the business world, it is readily acknowledged that even those solutions that seemed so creative on the drawing board may need reworking after they have been tested and evaluated. Similarly, agree with your family to come together after a trial period that is appropriate to the problem and the children's ages. If the topic is the scheduling of the family car by parents and teenagers, you may decide to discuss the issue again at the end of a month. But if you wait a month to talk about the project on bedroom conditions with your five-year-old, the effort is lost. You'll probably find yourself again maintaining order by periodic fireworks which leave everyone feeling (and acting) vengeful or guilty.

At this confab, see if everyone has done what they agreed to do, observing all time limits and other qualifications. Is the initial problem area being dealt with to the satisfaction of all?

Have any components of the agreement proved in practice to be unwieldy? Is anyone dissatisfied with the program? What adjustments need to be made? One family negotiated a reassignment of household duties. With four children of elementary school age and one infant, the mother balked at having to make all of the beds each day. But the rest of the family disliked her nagging. In a move that was no doubt motivated by generosity but faulted by unreality, the father agreed to assume the chore. Needless to say, he was ready to reassess the situation at the end of the week.

If there are basic problems with the contracts you originally designed, you will need to repeat the entire process. On the other hand, simple adjustments may be sufficient. The issue may have been one that could be remedied by the awareness and sensitivity promoted by the process. For example, all may agree on a schedule for television viewing that gives the children a range of choice but insures a reasonable bedtime, thus allowing the parents some time for themselves at the end of the day. Children seldom realize by themselves that their parents need this time. Pointing it out, in addition to planning together ways to get this time, helps them to become more aware and tolerant of the need. And, of course, the parents get their wish, too. Thus, periodic evaluations will generally become unnecessary as the problem ceases to exist.

If the contract is being ignored, however, consider the possibility that the real issue is not the problem as it was originally stated. If mealtime arguments over hated vegetables and wasted food continue (despite the formulation of creative options that seem to respond to all objections) it is probable that the real issue is either power or independence. No three-year-old will declare that she is establishing her separateness from her parents by refusing to eat carrots. But if working together to balance her preference and your need not to waste food do not help, you all may be playing complementary roles in the game called, "Watch what happens when I refuse to eat this!" You can refuse to play your parts by ignoring the ruckus or by dealing with it in such a way that it doesn't disturb you. But don't base your assessment of the feasibility of family negotiating on this experience. Wait until you've tried it on an issue that is uncomplicated by assorted undercurrents and hidden motivations.

And when you've successfully involved the family in this process, give yourself a hand. Bask in the glow that accompanies those moments of peace when everybody is satisfied. Not only are one set of interlocking problems solved, but you've worked together to do it. These are the moments that make family life worth the effort it takes.

Familylab

Why? To enable families to draw on the talents and resources of each member to find solutions to problems to which all contribute and for which all are responsible; to practice using our imagination in approaching a variety of situations.

When/Where? You will need adequate time for the complete working through of each step. That amount will depend on the age of your children; older children will be able to discuss more at length than younger ones. In any event, you will need to plan a time and place that is quiet and uninterrupted by television programs, phone calls, and other distractions which pull attention from the project itself.

The following activity may be done as a game by itself, or it may be done to deal with minor problems that arise on a daily basis. You may play with it at the supper table, or try it at other times when you have only a few minutes.

How: This exercise deals with brainstorming, a part of the longer process described in this chapter. We are usually so intent on finding immediate solutions to problems that we neglect the primary steps that could widen our perception of the issue or help us to approach the problem in truly creative ways.

1. Choose an imaginary situation or a minor problem area that actually exists in your family. For example, what is a perfect family like? Or how many ways are there of managing all of the afterschool trips that are needed every Wednesday afternoon? If need be, set a goal for your idea list. Agree to list at least 25 options, whether you think they would work or not. List everyone's contribution; don't censor any of them, since all of them may contain at least a suggestion of a solution to the problem.

Whether you actually complete the process of decision, implementation, and assessment on this topic is up to you. The important part of this activity is the practice it gives you in stretching your imagination so that all manner of alternatives can be considered.

Chapter 10

Inherited Marriage Roles and Parenting Patterns

Sherry: "Let's play 'House,' I'll be the mother, and you can be my little girl."

Cindy: "OK."

Sherry: "OK. You be upstairs, and I'm down here fixing breakfast."

Cindy: "OK. And . . ."

Sherry: "Daughter! Daughter! It's time to get up.

Get down here right now before it gets cold."

Cindy: "Well, . . ."

Sherry: "Hurry up. I have all these trips to do today—the grocery and . . . all these places. And you are making me late. You are a bad girl."

Cindy: "But . . ."

Sherry: "What will I do with you? You are *always*

slow and making me late. I will tell your father!"

Cindy: **"This isn't any fun. I think it's a dumb game, and I'm not going to play 'House' with you any more."**

1. Are there some factors in your present parenting or partnering that originated in your own experience of your parents and your observation of their behavior?

2. Which of those patterns do you find valuable and helpful?

3. Are there any that you don't agree with but find yourself doing anyway?

Over a mid-morning cup of coffee, my neighbor confided, "There are some things that my mother used to say to me that I swore I would *never* say to *my* children. You know, like "How can you girls fight with each other on your way home from church?" and "If you don't eat everything on your plate now, you will have to sit there until you do," or "You're so irresponsible that you'd lose your head if it weren't connected to you." But when I'm pushed to the wall, those are the things I say. The other day, I heard Jennie scolding the baby, and she sounded just like me—saying all those things I promised myself I would never say."

As important as our family relationships are to us, we move into them with little preparation and planning. We may conjure for ourselves vignettes of the birth of our children, the purchasing of our first house, and other such important moments. Ultimately, however, the dream we cherish before the wedding is usually at least somewhat different from the reality.

Even our ability to dream about our future is limited by the pressures of beginning a new life with someone. "We worried a lot about whether the wedding flowers would arrive on time or whether we had remembered to thank Aunt Marie and whether our reservations had been confirmed. But I don't remember ever realizing that my life was going to be different, until there it was—different," said another neighbor.

Although there is a trend toward later marriages, allowing both partners to develop an independent sense of accomplishment and purpose first, there is still bound to be some apprehension. Thornton Wilder's Dr. Gibbs confides his prenuptial fears to his wife: "Julia, I was afraid we wouldn't have material for conversation more'n'd last us a few weeks. I was afraid we'd run out and eat our meals in silence, that's a fact."[1]

And so, because new patterns represent a risk, and because we ourselves stand as evidence that the patterns of our childhood home, for all their faults, ultimately were successful, we tend to build our families around the ones we experienced as children. As one parent remarked to me at a program on family involvement in religious education, "How do I know that this way is better; after all, the old way worked on me."

In the final analysis, however, family relationships are too important to be left unexamined. The patterns and premises we learned when we were growing up may be those we finally choose for our own present relationships but we want to be able to choose them ourselves. This task is a difficult one although the results cannot be anything but rewarding and beneficial.

At the outset, however, there are several misconceptions that seem to be generally held despite any experience we have had to the contrary. The first is that all families are perfect. For example, as I officiate at our own mealtime chaos of vegetable confrontations, spilled milk, and pieces of adult conversation interrupted by children's gossip and arguments, I have the hunch that my neighbors' tables are serene and orderly. My fantasy of their mealtimes includes white tablecloths (that are used all week without a spot), plates that are cleared without a single wrinkled nose or resounding "Aggh!" and coherent discussions that serve as education

---

[1] Thornton Wilder, *Three Plays by Thornton Wilder* (New York: Harper and Row, Publishers, 1957), "Our Town", Act 2.

and stimulation for all. When nightfall finds me damp and exhausted from the bathing and bedding down routine, I imagine their children, clean on command, moving decorously through night prayers and goodnight hugs to immediate slumber. Their children never fight, their wives never have difficulty balancing the checkbooks, and their husbands never forget to fill their gas tanks.

But there is no such thing as a "perfect" family, and our efforts to create one will be doomed to failure. "I was always jealous of my neighbors," a friend of mind confided. "Whenever I was at their house, their kids were always so mannerly that I cringed to compare them with mine. I was actually relieved the day that one of them got in a fight." One of the most helpful outcomes of parent education courses is the reassurance that living in family is not easy, that each family has its ups **and** downs.

The second windmill at which we aim our lance is inconsistency. "Once two people get married, they cease to have different values and opinions," says the voice I would like to believe. And so, on top of the anger, frustration, impatience and other emotions that accompany family altercations, I also feel guilty and afraid. After all, the script isn't supposed to go that way. If it does, where did I fail? And is this the beginning of the end of the relationship?

People are not consistent. We change moods from minute to minute, even on a good day. Today, I can laugh when I discover my toddler in the act of creating a mud masterpiece; tomorrow he may receive a spanking. Today I can take it in stride if my husband forgets to tell me that he will be late for supper or if my wife lost the most recent bank deposit receipt. Tomorrow, there may be fireworks over the same situation.

If individuals vary in their feelings and convictions, then it is also reasonable to expect that they will vary in their demands on their children. Some behavior that seems allowable to one parent will irritate the other, and what one parent would punish may seem blameless to the other. Presenting a united front under any circumstances is unrealistic. To ignore differences means that the children will eventually learn to work the parents against each other to get what they want,

while the parents proclaim—with a grimace—that they do
agree. Conversely, admitting a difference in standards opens
the issue to negotiation; surely there are enough options that
each person in the transaction can be heard and satisfied.

The chances are that we labor under those two misconceptions because of the parenting patterns we observed and
experienced as children. The native intuition of children being
what it is, we probably knew when our parents disagreed o
when they were under some stress, even if we were not told
about it. But children must be protected from such problems
and complexities, said the style of the day, and so we have
come now to think of our present experience in unrealistic
terms. Parents disagree with each other and children need to
be able to adjust to that openly and honestly. When open
difference of opinion isn't allowed "in front of the children,"
they soon learn to manipulate matters to their advantage.

Ironically, disagreements and other grains of sand in the
family machinery do not disappear when they are confined
behind the scenes. If I raise my voice the first time the baby
splashes me with oatmeal, the problem may not escalate to
the point where I commit mayhem. Hell hath no fury like the
righteous person who has been patient, forbearing, and silent
in adversity.

In addition to those two patterns which are a common
legacy, we receive other assorted scripts and directives for
relating with partner and children. What injunctions did you
receive regarding neatness, for example? An untidy house
reflects on the quality of the mother's love for her family, says
one directive. Masculinity and housework are incompatible,
says another. But it's nice when someone shares the
responsibility, says our experience. Thus, it is difficult to
balance feeling inadequate and inappropriate with wanting
help with a task.

Never be taken in by someone else, says a warning voice
from the past. People are out to get you. "Some of us in the
neighborhood are forming a babysitting pool," says a
neighbor. "If you'd like to have a morning off each week,
you're welcome to join." How do I balance both?

Children's behavior reflects on their parents, says that

voice. "Your son and mine always want to play together," says the mother next door. "But as soon as they're together, they quarrel." How do I respond, without making my child the victim of my defensiveness?

Cleanliness is next to godliness. The husband is the head of the family. An outspoken, forward woman is the ruination of her husband's success as head of the family. Masculinity and tenderness are incompatible. Never be late. Spare the rod and spoil the child. The list of such injunctions is endless. Some may contain a particle of truth. All of them involve feelings that are related to our concern for our families and our determination to be good marriage partners and parents. But unless we carefully examine these instructions that we have picked up in our past, we will be caught between our feelings and our common sense. This Familylab offers one approach to that examination.

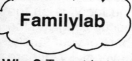

Familylab

Why? To get in touch with these aspects of our behavior as family members which are based in the experience of family that we had as children.

When/Where? Allow at least 30 minutes for this fantasy each time it is done. You may wish to do it with your spouse, in which case a sharing of the insights each has discovered would be a useful conclusion to the exercise.

How? Arrange for a time and place where you can relax and enjoy complete quiet and freedom from distraction. Find a comfortable position and close your eyes. Take a few minutes to pay attention to your breathing, visualizing the air as it flows through your body, in and out. Imagine that as it surges through your limbs it washes out all of the tensions you have collected during the day. Watch them as they gather and flow out with the exhaled breaths.

When you are totally relaxed, imagine that you visit your

childhood home. If you remember several, choose the home that meant the most to you. Begin at the corner, and walk up to your house. Take some time to look at the house, noticing as many details as you can. Then go up to the front door. Enter, and walk through the rooms slowly, being careful to watch for details. Who is in the house with you? What do they look like? What are they doing? Spend some time observing these people.

Next, choose one area of family operation in your childhood home. It may be discipline, family prayer, parenting role assignments, recreation, finances, attitudes toward work or education, conduct during mealtimes, behavior toward "company," treatment of sex, or any of the categories of interaction between various family members. Take some time to watch a typical transaction in the area you chose—a mealtime, a punishment or a money dealing, for example. Concentrate on the roles of your parents. It doesn't matter if the specific incident took place or not. The focus is on the manner in which it probably would have occurred, given the personalities and convictions of the members of your family. What are your parents saying? How do they look? What are their gestures saying? What part are you playing in the drama?

When you have played to the end of the segment, leave the room and the house and open your eyes. Take several minutes to reflect on what you have just seen and experienced. If you have done this with your spouse, share whatever points you wish. Then talk together about how you see the behavior and mannerisms of your parents reflected in your own present behavior. Be as specific as you can, especially in the feedback you are able to give your partner. We sometimes aren't aware of the image we present until someone alerts us to it.

How do you feel about this input? Are there points that you would like to change or replace in your behavior? What would you like to reinforce?

You may do this exercise a number of times, each time with a different aspect of your experience of your parents.

Suggested Reading

Bernard, Jessie. *The Future of Marriage.* New York: World Publishing Company, 1972.
This is a good survey of the subject, despite the textbook approach. Deals with authority and role assignment, among other topics.

Bird, Joseph and Lois. *Marriage is For Grown-ups.* Garden City: Doubleday and Co., 1969.
Excellent, dealing with communication, finances, sex, in-laws, children, faith, job demands, and problem drinking.

Bolles, Richard N. *What Color Is Your Parachute?* Berkeley: Ten-speed Press, 1972.
Utilization of techniques for self-knowledge in the process of job hunting and career selection.

Cultural Information Service New York: CIStems, Inc., P.O. Box 92, New York, N.Y. 10016.
This monthly magazine is a review of the arts and media, with discussion guides on current films, records, paperbacks and television offerings. Invaluable for family processing of programs, and especially helpful if you'd like some help in discussing popular records with your teenagers.

Dreikurs, Rudolf. *Coping with Children's Misbehavior: A Parent's Guide.* New York: Hawthorn Books, Inc., 1972.
This is an abridged edition of The Challenge of Parenthood, an approach to family living that considers the value and rights of all members.

Dreikurs, Dr. Rudolf; Shirley Gould, and Dr. Raymond Corsini. *Family Council.* Chicago: Henry Regnery Co., 1974.
Subtitled, "The Dreikurs Technique for putting an end to war between parents and children (and between children

and children)," this approach uses a family meeting format for dealing with disagreements and trouble spots in daily living.

Ellis, Albert and Robert Harper. *Creative Marriage.* New York: Lyle Stuart, 1961.
Called a "self-help book on marriage, based on couples' ability to look at themselves and take appropriate action." Emphasis on sexual relationship between partners; also discusses in-law problems, children, etc.

Glasser, William. *The Identity Society.* New York: Harper and Row, Publishers, 1972.
Develops the theory that after World War II, Western culture moved from goal orientation to role or identity orientation. Suggests plans for institutional change and for family communication.

Laing, R.D. *The Politics of the Family.* New York: Pantheon Books, 1971.
Illustrates the approach to families as systems by describing the involvement of entire family units in the treatment of the "illness" of one member.

Rogers, Carl. *Becoming Partners.* New York: Dell Publishing Company, Inc., 1972.
A collection of interviews with couples representing a wide variety of marriage forms, with reflections by Rogers.

Satir, Virginia. *Peoplemaking.* Palo Alto: Science and Behavior Books, Inc., 1972.
Warmly written analysis of self-worth, communication, systems and rules in the family setting, with exercises for family use.

Steiner, Claude. *Scripts People Live.* New York: Grove
   Press, Inc., 1974.
   *Explanation of Transactional Analysis as applied to life
   scripts. Applications to family processes.*

PART THREE

THE FAMILY'S RELIGIOUS AWARENESS

Chapter 8

Developing Personal Faith

"Arlo says, 'Every poet flashes, at some time in his life. And then he sees the infinite. The perception is a gift.' Has Guthrie also seen it? I'm a musician, not a painter. I've heard it,' he replies.

He does not proselytize or preach. He avoids reciting dogma. He says he's 'Catholic-Jewish' and does not explain further. Has he experienced a conversion? 'It's nothing like that,' he says.

I see what you say
and I
hear what you don't

'We're in an interesting situation. Most of us, I figure, don't know if we're religious, or atheists, or not. You can't live without confusion, not in a world like ours. But then something happens. I don't know how to tell you. I know that something yanked me—it was not of my own doing. It's like being thrown in water when you don't know how to swim. If you learn to paddle, wonderful. If you drown, why, that's a shame.' "

"Arlo Guthrie at 30"
Paul Richard, *The Washington Post,* July 29, 1977

70

1. *Is your present religious affiliation the same as that of your childhood?*

2. *Was rebellion against religious structures and/or values a part of your adolescence?*

3. *What role does faith play in your present life?*

4. *Is that related to your religious affiliation or member-ship in a particular denomination?*

5. *Have you experienced a development in your faith?*

6. *Have you observed a development in the faith of your children?*

I'm certain it was coincidence that in one of my recent family communication classes, at least one of every two partners was professionally involved in some health service—nursing, dietetics, dental hygiene, etc. With that background, however, it was not coincidence that mealtime behavior of their children quickly became a favorite issue, one that we returned to class after class as we dealt with various skills. Over the weeks, the participants themselves intellectualized about the harm of forcing their children to eat everything on their plates, the dubious food value of "just two more bites of carrot," and the problems of adult obesity begun by such injunctions in childhood. Nevertheless, at the conclusion of the course, most of the parents said that, first, they could admit that the issue was one of values, and second, they would probably continue to impose their values in that area. They might be willing to act as consultants to their children on a host of other issues but not on this one.

The issue of mealtime rules was important to this particular group because of their professional backgrounds as well as their roles as parents. But had I (wearing my hat as a religious educator) taught the course in a church setting, the issue might just as well have been the transmission of religious values or the passing down of their faith to their children.

The term "Faith" has a wide variety of meanings. First, it can be understood as a body of beliefs. For Roman Catholics for whom faith is popularly equated with doctrine, this faith is generally understood as being transmitted by parish-sponsored classes for children. Historically, uniformity of content was insured for American Catholics by the use of the *Baltimore Catechism,* which consisted of a series of questions and answers which were memorized by the students. The same sequence was retaught each year with greater depth as the students advanced. The dryness of the material and the compulsory nature of the classes combined to make faith-as-doctrine an unpleasant study for many. But the sanctions that come into play when religion and God are involved meant that it was risky to question, to rebel. Consequently, while it is normal for a person's concept of God and religion to grow and change with the person's maturation in other areas, this is a source of much pain and confusion for adults whose experience seems removed from or at variance with deeply ingrained childhood learnings.

This has been the situation for denominations in which faith denotes a body of doctrinal definitions. In denominations in which such uniformity is not an issue, faith popularly means adherence to certain standards of conduct. During the bicentennial's flood of retrospection, there was much written on the peculiar bent of American religion in that direction.

Here having faith generally is taken as an indication of one's ethical standards, and so rearing one's children in religious matters means forming them in habits of regular church attendance, honesty, charitableness, and other virtues. In this context, one will hear remarks like, "He is a religious person . . . even though he doesn't go to church," as though it is puzzling that the two could go together.

A third school of thought sees faith in terms of relationship. Faith here is assent to participation in the life of God, freely given by God and responded to by man. Ethics and doctrine may flow from a commitment to this relationship; they do not constitute it any more than agreements about finances and definitions of life style constitute a marriage. And in fact, for Scripture writers and mystics, this understanding of faith was analogous to the relationship between marriage partners. To continue with that image, marriage relationships are not static. They grow as the individuals grow in their ability to love each other and as their various motivations for being together deepen. Similarly, faith is a developing process in that one's ability to grasp the content of religious belief and one's motivations for believing change and deepen. According to James Fowler, a researcher in this area of faith development, there are stages through which people gradually move. In other words, we believe the way we do at various stages because of the way we perceive our relationship to the world. We grow through various sets of images in which our faith is expressed.

In the earliest stages of childhood, the world is an uncomplicated place, and so children assume that the universe is unified and free of problems. Needs usually are met quickly. Difficulties are explained away easily. For example, when my little sister surprised my parents in the act of decorating the Christmas tree which she believed Santa Claus was to have brought, she accused them of trying to take the credit that belonged to him. It didn't occur to her to question his existence—until the following year.

But this idyllic worldview develops cracks when children become aware of places where harmony and disunity do not reign undisputed. They even may realize that their parents sometimes disagree or quarrel, or they may experience the death of a grandparent, friend or pet. Since their survival needs at this age are still great, it is too risky to admit the possibility of unanswered questions or chaos. And since their resources outside the home are still relatively few at this age, their only recourse is to place complete trust in parents. This is the "good boy-good girl" stage; seldom again will the rulings of the parents be so scrupulously observed with so little questioning or hesitation.

Then, even in the best of families, it soon becomes apparent that there are other authorities. The child's horizons widen and there are others who are able to answer needs and impose order on confusion. There are teachers, popular neighborhood or community figures, even television heroes.

But sometimes **they** disagree, and the anxiety that began to be felt in each of the other periods is felt again. Now, the safest thing is to place one's faith in the community. Children at this stage like to go to church; the religious rituals reassure them that there is some way of controlling disorder.

By adolescence, there are hints that even the community—church, school, social groups, etc—will not replace a person's own need to sort through various beliefs and values. Now, in the struggle to find personal faith, earlier principles are set aside at least temporarily. Depending on their ability to trust their children and their need to maintain control, the parents may find these declarations of independence rather hard to take. But it is just as difficult for the adolescent to negotiate this time of searching, and patient support is most helpful.

Conflict is a fact of life, and even despite a person's strongest commitment to a set of values, issues will continue to be complex and decisions will continue to be painful at times. This realization may be the outcome of the adolescent's searching. Or, if that is too difficult to accept, the person will retreat to one of the external authorities of the previous periods as a source of security. But if one is able to live with the ambiguities of life, gradually a new unity emerges. It is akin to the tranquility despite daily bustling that Gail Sheehy (in her book *Passages*) associates with the successful passage through the mid-life crisis. Despite all, God is present as a center of meaning, not so much as the force that keeps chaos at bay.

All of this is not to deny the belief that faith is a gift from God. But the truism that "Grace builds on nature" is applicable here. A child's faith is conditioned by physical, psychological and emotional states which, of course, change as the child matures.

Nevertheless, it is difficult to allow those we love to experience doubt or to reject values or doctrinal tenets that we believe. "After all," we reason, "they've worked for **me.**" We forget that they "work" precisely because we were allowed to grow into them at some point, so that they flow from our particular experience with God and our world.

It is fairly certain then, that forcing abstract dogmatic formulas on children is not conducive to their growth in faith. When this is done, the child naturally equates faith with parental authority, and the struggle for independence that takes place during adolescence then involves both issues. Rather, religious formation should include calm exchanges about what is believed both by parent and child. Challenges which parents interpret as obstinacy are usually in fact initially honest questions. For example, the youngster's question about "Why do I have to go to church," nearly always means "Why do you go; what do you get from going?" An angry response can logically be interpreted as, "I don't know, but it's dangerous for both of us to ask that question."

Religious customs and rituals are the arena where many of these questions originate, and parents should be prepared to explain why they do things a particular way, both at home and at church. For instance, the use of blessings at church can be mirrored in beautiful family blessings at home, in which parents communicate their faith in God and their care for each other. But parents should be prepared to explain what they believe about such a service.

Perhaps things were easier and less complicated when we believed that faith was a one-step acceptance of a whole package. Life itself is a process, however, and faith is a matter of growth in the ability to trust. This Familylab offers an opportunity to think together about our faith and the beliefs which flow from the relationship with God.

Familylab

Why? To examine the beliefs that give shape to our faith.

When/Where? The first activity is an aid to adult reflection, and requires some quiet time. The second is for a family discussion; allow 30 minutes to an hour, depending on the age and size of the group.

How? 1. a) In writing, complete this statement: "I believe . . ."

b) Then write down as clearly as possible why you hold this belief.

c) Looking at your "Why" answer, formulate another belief statement related to that answer. For example, "I believe that Jesus is God because of the evidence of Scripture. I believe that what is written in the Scriptures is true because . . ."

d) Again, ask yourself why you hold that belief.

e) Repeat this until you have no more "Why" answers. Is this the central issue of your faith?

2. a) Together, think of someone whom you love very much. Write that person's name on a piece of paper.

b) How did you meet? Describe the meeting in a few sentences.

c) Think about the person, recalling as much as you can about your relationship. Then write out your reasons for loving the person.

d) Many opportunities and situations have brought you from your initial meeting to today when you can say you love this person very much. Write a paragraph or so about how this happened, how you grew in love.

e) Does this knowing and loving the person have an effect on your life? Describe the effect on who you are, how you act, how you live, as accurately as possible.

f) Go back and slowly reread from the beginning what you have written. Change whatever needs changing as you reflect more deeply on your answers.

g) If you wish, share what you have written with a person of your choosing.

h) Reflect on what has been written and spoken, and especially on the effect which doing this exercise may have had.

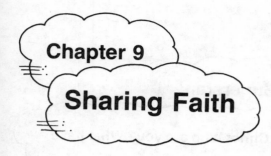

Chapter 9

Sharing Faith

The Sounds of Silence

And the people bowed and prayed
To the neon god they made,
And the sign burst out its warning,
In the words that it was forming,
And the sign said: "The words of the
prophets are written
on the subway walls,
And tenement halls,
And whisper in the sounds of silence."

Paul Simon
Charing Cross Music Company

Jesus Christ Superstar

Jesus Christ Jesus Christ Who are you? What have you sacrificed?
Jesus Christ Superstar Do you think you're what they say you are?

Andrew Lloyd Webber, Tim Rice
Leeds Music Corp.

Mass-Credo

I believe in God,
But does God believe in me?
I'll believe in any god
If any god there be . . .
I believe in one God,
But then I believe in three.
I'll believe in twenty gods
If they'll believe in me.

Stephen Schwartz, Leonard Bernstein
G. Schirmer, Inc.

1. What is your faith?

2. What is the faith of the other members of your family?

3. Have you ever discussed this with them as a discussion participant rather than instructor?

4. How would you react to your teenager's declaration that s/he is an atheist?

5. If your spouse belongs to a different religious denomination or is not affiliated with a church, how do you deal with this?

6. How have you explained this to your children?

The word, "faith," has an interesting and revealing etymology. It has its roots in the Indo-European group of words meaning "to persuade, compel, confide." In Latin, this became specifically "to trust," while in the Germanic languages, two definitions are traced to the original: "To await trustingly," and "treaty" or "league."[1] Faith is assent to the beginning premise that there is some ultimate meaning to our lives. In other words, my faith is my conviction that there is a God who shares His Life with us. The particular shape that faith takes is belief.

It is a common error to equate the two. Faith is incorrectly identified with one's denominational affiliation or the specific tenets or beliefs of a particular church. At a parish meeting, for example, one of the participants spoke of her "faith" in the Virgin Birth. But to equate faith with belief is to fail to see faith as a continuing search to find meaning in one's life and the world. Faith is a process; beliefs are milestones along the way.

In this framework, then, belief has several characteristics.

---

[1] *American Heritage Dictionary of the English Language.* (New York: Houghton Mifflin Co.) 1969.

Belief takes various forms. It is not limited to theological formulations, but may be found in the creations of artists and poets who give shape to the intuitions and wonderings of people on the relationship between God and the world. There is the triumphalism of a Michelangelo painting or the pessimism and shock of Picasso's "Guernica"; both are expressions of specific beliefs.

Second, beliefs are not statements which float freely around the heavens. They are linked to personal experience. For example, a belief in God as Father necessarily relies heavily for its meaning on the individual's experience of fathering and being fathered. For some, the image of fatherhood may not be a suitable one to embody the creative power and concern of a caring God.

Finally, beliefs are set in a particular cultural and historical milieu. Again, the contemporary emphasis on sexual equality and women's rights makes fatherhood an inappropriate image for many. Our faith may be in God whose love is always available to us, whose willingness to share life with us is dependent only on our willingness to participate in it. Our **belief** is that God is Creator or Punisher or Accountant or Lover. In terms of the etymology, faith is acceptance of the reality of God; beliefs are the specific tenets of the treaty, the specific forms of the trust.

So belief is never static. It is always a reflection of experience. In that connection, orthodoxy or adherence to the beliefs taught by a particular church, is a guide. We have statements by previous generations of **their** beliefs, and as such, these serve as valuable guides. But because beliefs use the images of specific cultures and historical periods, they must be constantly open to reinterpretation and assimilation by new generations. Problems arise when, again, specific beliefs and images are guarded and solidified.

For example, several months ago my colleague and I gave a workshop for a group of parents and religious educators. During the discussion on Eucharist we saw a variety of beliefs, all of them within the limits of orthodoxy in the Roman Catholic tradition. In discussing the format for the approaching parish celebration of First Reception of the Eucharist, some parents wished their children to wear the traditional suits and white dresses and to be seated by themselves in the front pews of the church. This was consistent with the concept of Eucharist as sacred, distant, and individual—"me and God."

Other parents took pride in involving the entire family in the preparation of their children for the sacrament, and took many opportunities to draw parallels between the Eucharist and family meals. For them, the actual First Communion seemed most appropriate in the context of a home Mass or when the entire parish demonstrated unity with the children. They wanted their children to sit as families, and considered such forms of celebration as a parish reception to follow the Mass. This was equally orthodox, consistent with a communitarian view of the Eucharist.

Both views could find support in Catholic practice and theology as well as in the personal experience of the participants. Thus, the question that so many ask, "But what does the Church teach," is a moot point. Truth is always a reflection rather than a dictation. And truth is always a reflection of experience, not a static definition of the specific form which the "Mind of God" is assumed to have taken.

In this connection, there is often (especially for Catholics) a confusion between discipline and doctrine. "What does the Church teach?" in the context of a discussion on faith and beliefs often means, "What do we have to **do?**" rather than "What do we have to believe?" Catholics who rebel against contemporary developments in the Church most often cite their discomfort with Mass in the vernacular language or the elimination of Friday abstinence from meat. "People used to know you were Catholic because you had to watch what you ate on Fridays," they say with a touch of nostalgic regret. "Now we're no better than everybody else," they sadly add.

So our past understanding said that a Catholic was somebody who went to hell if dying immediately following a Friday steak. In contrast, there was the official reaction to the matter of Archbishop Lefevbre. The response of Pope Paul VI to the archbishop's threats and ultimate action of ordaining priests in the Tridentine tradition was sorrow and pleading.

But even when the action was accomplished, the word "excommunication" was not mentioned by the Pope. In previous ages, the dissidents would have been excommunicated promptly and, depending on the political ramifications and Papal armies, perhaps executed. But now, our notion of God—our beliefs—will no longer allow us to put discipline in the arena of faith. God is no longer defined in our social and theological milieu as "He who enforces Church Law."

So doctrine is the witness of the past, a statement of the reflection of others as it was tested and found to be helpful in interpreting human experience. But as experience changes, continuing reflection is vital. Thus, the task of parents is primarily not to teach doctrine but to enable reflection. Children ask, "Who is God?" and "What happens to us when we die?" and "Why do I have to go to Church?" If our answers spring from our unquestioning acceptance of doctrine, we will sound defensive. Our answers will seem unreasonable, and religion will be an ideal arena for the teenage rebellion that could as easily center on other less crucial topics.

Recently, *The Washington Post* ran a feature on an Orthodox Jewish family. The parents were highly educated and quite wealthy, the article pointed out, thus countering the argument that faith is the refuge of the poor, uneducated, and superstitious. The family lived three and one half miles from the synagogue and with an infant and a toddler, made the roundtrip by foot each Sabbath. The reporter dwelt on the inconveniences necessitated by the family's strict adherence to Orthodox discipline—three sets of dishes for kosher food, business travel arrangements around the Sabbath prohibitions, planning heating and lighting ahead to avoid the use of switches during the Sabbath, etc. The account culminated with this paragraph:

> With the impositions Adie and I have faced, we could have walked away from our faith long ago if we'd wanted to. But where is Adam going to stand if we continue living in a place like we are now, and don't make a super-valiant effort for our religion? . . . Where are his friends going to be? Where is he going to find an Orthodox girl, someone who

will conform to his way? I feel that if we teach him the positive things about his religion, let him ask questions, get him involved—that counts for an awful lot.[1]

Familylab

Why? To enable the family members to examine their own faith, seeing the connection between their experience and their faith; to engage the family members in sharing the insights received through this reflection with each other.

When/Where? The first of the following three exercises will require up to an hour for the preliminary discussion, depending on the age of your children and the scope of the discussion. The celebration which you design will be held later, the time to be decided as part of the planning. The second can be done as a follow-up to a discussion, or as an activity by itself, especially with younger children. Since our concept of God changes and develops, it may be done more than once. The fantasy described in the third activity may be done more than once, again depending on the ages of the participants. For this exercise, it is necessary to find a time and place that will be absolutely quiet and free of all noise and pressure, with room for everyone to spread out comfortably. Sounds like dripping faucets and background music which we ordinarily have become accustomed to can be a distraction during this type of meditation.

How? 1. Suppose that you were to develop an alternative to the regular form of worship in which you usually participate. For example, especially if some members of your family claim that Mass is not "their way" of praying, what **is** a way of praying together that all of you find satisfying?

---

[1]Janis Johnson, "Families Obey Ancient Law With Sabbath Trek" (Washington, D.C. The Washington Post Publishing Company) July 3, 1977.

Here it may be necessary to clarify the difference between public and private prayer and to talk about the need for both. While most of us would agree that a crowded noisy church is not as conducive to private prayer as a quiet shady park, some of those sounds and "distractions" may even enhance a community prayer service. This exercise concerns communal prayer forms, with the understanding that private prayer is also necessary and enriching.

2. In addition, again with older children, you may discuss community prayer as a time when we share our faith and celebrate our relationship with each other and with God. This means that you will probably confront the notion of Sunday churchgoing as a matter of discipline. Your discussion may center on ways in which your family could make the Sunday church experience more meaningful. Suggestions might include looking up the readings and using one or another of the passages for a family prayer service during the week. A Sunday family discussion about the sermon—perhaps even on the way home from church—would help to make it relevant to your particular family. Members might enjoy a weekday home Mass or prayer service conducted by your minister so that they may ask questions about vestments and procedures.

3. Apart from these issues spend some time talking about what you think should take place during a worship service. How would you include those elements in a family service? What gestures would you plan in order to give shape to the ideas you wish to include? For example, would you include some time for the participants to ask forgiveness of each other for hurts given and received? How would you act that out? -a handshake or embrace? -crossing each person on the forehead?

Would you use readings or suggest items for discussion? What themes would be appropriate for your family service? What are some good sources for passages that would be conducive to reflection and prayer? Would you allow time for the family members to pray for each other or to ask for prayers for their own particular needs?

What setting would embody the themes you've chosen? You may plan a family meal, for which each person prepares some part of the food, and where the conversation centers on a reading and the conclusion is the prayer service itself. You may have your service at bedtime or on a Sunday morning. Within a day or so after the service, talk about whether it was a helpful form of praying together for your family. With that evaluation, you are ready to plan another service.

During this discussion, the adult temptation is to **teach** about God, whether your instructions reflect your present convictions or your memories of your childhood religion lessons. Instead, **model** reflection by working through this exercise for your own benefit rather than because "It will be good for the children."

4. Who is God? Depending on the age and propensities of the family members, you may work on this question by making a collage, gluing to a large sheet of paper cutout pictures and captions from magazines and newspapers that contribute to a definition of God. Or you may make a list together. Each person around the family circle adds one item until you have run out of answers.

Chapter 10

Prayer

"All right, everybody. Time to get quiet. We're going to say our prayers. Susan, kneel down. No pinching! Jerry, fold your hands. Who wants to start? O.K. Susan, you begin. No, Jerry. You can

begin tomorrow. Let's be serious. We speak to God with respect instead of giggling. O.K. 'Our Father . . . 'Jerry! '. . . and lead us . . .' God bless . . . Isn't there anyone else we should pray for? No, Susan. We don't pray for the Tooth Fairy. Yes, I'm sure that Grandpa is happy that we prayed for him . . ."

1. *How would you define prayer?*

2. *How is that related to your definition of God?*

3. *How do your children define prayer?*

4. *Do you pray with your children?*

It seems strange to say, "We used to . . ." about prayer, the timelessness of God and our need for Him being what it is. Nevertheless, the popular conception of prayer is changing and we are more comfortable now with types of prayer that would have felt strange to us even a few years ago.. For instance, as we become more willing to reflect on our experience as a basis for our theologizing and praying, we are more at ease with praying in our own words, without the use of formulas. Studies of various cultures are providing a basis for exploring the ways in which they can enrich our prayer. For example, Yoga and Zen have found their way into contemporary Western prayer forms.

Despite our own developing notions of prayer, however, the chances are that we instruct our children in the same patterns and formulas we learned as children. Generally, that means that we teach them the Prayer Before Meals and a Prayer For Forgiveness for bedtimes. If this has been their orientation to prayer, we cannot be surprised at some of the conclusions they draw. At a family workshop, I asked family units to spend some time together defining prayer. One very conscientious couple were stunned when their children said, "Prayer is something you do when you are little; when you grow up, you don't have to do it any more." Nevertheless, when prayer is a children's activity which adults supervise but in which they do not participate, this conclusion is the only logical one children can draw.

While the Christian churches often have seemed to be distrustful of human experience, Yoga and Zen both strive for an integration of body and mind with the God to whom we pray. The hope is that this experience of wholeness, of the lack of separateness and categorization, will lead to a transformation of life, to a glimpse of the essential unity of God and man.

In family living, however, we usually erect sharp barriers between the various types of activities. We feel that some are religious; some clearly are not. We interrupt important family moments for the sake of those we define as more properly prayerful. For example, Sunday morning with younger children is often a time for cuddling with a father or mother who isn't at home on weekday mornings. It is a time when feelings of security, warmth and intimacy replace the impatience and peremptoriness of pressured weekday transactions. The nurturing comes to an abrupt halt, however, so that the family can make it to church on time. Children aren't the only ones whose prayer life suffers when we cut these moments short.

Or meal prayers: parents declare, "Quiet while we say grace," in the fervent hope that all combatants and disgruntled diners will forget their disputes during the hiatus. One can't imagine Jesus similarly presiding at a meal at which his apostles argue about who shall sit at his right hand in the Kingdom or puzzle about why their efforts at curing people aren't uniformly successful with, "Everybody be quiet now! Peter, it's your turn today. Say the words nice and clear so we can understand them." Instead, he dealt with questions and arguments when they occurred; they weren't seen merely as interruptions.

Family living is itself a religious process. For better or for worse, our image of God flows from our experience of family, and the concerns we bring to our formal prayer often center on the needs of our family or ourselves as family members. Within that context, prayer will take various shapes. Each is appropriate at one time or another, and we initiate our children to each style by modeling it, by praying with them and by allowing them to "eavesdrop" on our prayers just as we join theirs. Teaching them about prayer, in the same sense as we teach them what to do in case of an emergency or instruct them in how to keep their bedrooms neat does give the impression that we ourselves are a certain distance from it. Whether our prayer is private or communal, impromptu and spontaneous or worded in favorite formulas, we help them to pray by posing examples.

And what **is** prayer? First, prayer is an expression of wonder. A national engineering company is currently in the midst of a television advertising campaign; each TV "spot" begins with a "What if . . ." question. "What if there were a building that could calculate its own heating and cooling cycles? . . . That time is now!" the voice proclaims. Wonder is radical openness to all being: What if someone loves us no matter what, forever? That "if" is now! What if God's Spirit were ours, too? That time is now! Wonder is the willingness to believe in the wildest extent of our imagination. What if we really are all members of one Body? What if we really will live—forever?

In this context, prayer is the celebration of an amazing reality. Unfortunately, we often think of prayer as asking God to manipulate something for us so that we achieve a desired result: "Let the X-rays be clear," "Let me pass this test," and "In St. Anthony's name, dear God, please help me find those car keys."

But thinking in those terms is difficult to integrate with our experience of not always receiving what we ask for. In order to reason ourselves out of a corner, we tell ourselves that God doesn't answer all of our requests because
a) they probably aren't good for us in the long run anyway;
b) we shouldn't always be asking for specific things but rather for the ability to resign ourselves to what we **do** receive. None of this is convincing, especially if the stakes are high.

This stance assumes that God is "out there," and that our prayers of supplication are like cosmic telegrams to another Person. What if we could answer some of those requests ourselves? What if my prayers were answered at my creation when I was given the power to do those things for which I ask God to intervene now? Assuming that this wonder is now, prayer of petition is psychic problemsolving, allowing me the time to focus my attention and energy on issues that matter to me. Above all, this is consistent with my belief that while God is not limited to my being, he is certainly present in me and more than in a manner of speaking.

If this is true of prayers of petition, it is also true of contrition, adoration and thanksgiving. Does **God** need to hear me state those sentiments? Or do I need to hear myself say them? The other day I saw a bumper sticker that proclaimed, "Physics makes the world go around." Prayer then helps us to discover its meaning.

Dealing with prayer in the family begins with reflection. There are times during the day and week when this might happen naturally, if we allow it. For example, bedtimes, daily or weekly family meals, reconciliations, and family outings like picnics or vacations are times that might lend a few minutes to quiet thinking and talking about what has happened or is happening to the family and its members. Without this reflection, formulas are meaningless and community prayers, even if they are said in one's own words, make the participants uncomfortable and unpeaceful.

When we use the words of others for our prayers, they should fit our needs. The Psalms cover a whole range of feelings and thoughts not found in more popular prayers but their imagery often needs explanation and discussion, especially for younger children. Many of the parables make good starting points for sharing and spontaneous prayer. Again, if couples are comfortable with this themselves, they will have no difficulty developing this style in family prayer.

Just as we customarily think of prayer in terms of **saying** something rather than as reflection or action, we often neglect the possibilities that ritual holds for family prayer. Ritual is the celebration of those moments about which we have prayed in such a way that the meaning shines through to the community that celebrates with us. In ritual, we use our senses to recreate a moment so that its meaning can be experienced again and shared with those closest to us.

If those rituals which we usually associate with church liturgies are meaningless and fail to involve us, perhaps it is because we do not capitalize on parallel moments when they do occur most meaningfully for us—in our homes. Thus, reflection on the meaning of a family meal and celebration of that meaning underlies our understanding of Eucharist as the family meal of the church community. Anniversaries are occasions for sharing our thoughts on the marking of another year together. Perhaps it is only after years of that reflecting and celebrating in the home that the marriage vows make sense. "Is **that** what those promises meant?" declare the couple as they gaze around the family circle. "Well . . . we're happy about it; we'd do it again!" And the family rejoices in the **reality** of the marriage, not merely the promise to try to make one.

Reconciliation is an enriching experience, wherever it takes place. But nowhere is it likely to be as needed or as much in touch with the reality of faults and rough spots as in the home. It was no particular problem for me to earn an "A" in Conduct at school, and weekly confession was easy. I was much less inhibited at home and reconciliations there were hard won. They should have had their own celebration. Celebrations of the periodic maturings that happen in the home are occasions for family prayer. New teeth, new bicycles, birthdays, bestowal of new privileges and responsibilities, new jobs (for children **and** parents), farewells, successful or unsuccessful negotiating of hurdles all need to be given form so that their meaning can be captured and savored by the family.

How can we explain the nature of prayer to children? "I don't want my children to get the impression that they can ask God for anything they want and He will automatically give to them," said one mother. In this context, the notion of **wish** is particularly fitting for two reasons. First, a wish is understood to be an expression of an attitude rather than a specific request. Children understand wishes in much the same way in which they understand the convention of story. Neither one is a literal matter; both reveal a greater truth. "I wish we will all be safe tonight," is an evening prayer of trust and faith, for example.

Second, prayer as wishing emphasizes the concept that God is **in here,** not solely "out there." The "out there" God is less relevant to our spending a night in peace than the God among us who enables us to care for each other. The God "out there" is not nearly so important in the providing of the material things for which we wish as the work that we ourselves do to achieve them, once we've centered our energy on it. The wondrous thing is that **we** care for each other.

Once we move past our misconceptions that prayer is for children, and that family life is little more than preparation for formal church worship, we will discover the riches that prayer holds in the family setting. This Familylab deals with one specific format for family prayer; more are suggested in the other chapters in this section.

Familylab

Why? To experience fantasy as a form of prayer which can be equally meaningful for adults as well as children.

When/Where? Allow about 30 minutes as a minimum for this activity, depending on the age and attention span of the participants. Plan a place that is free from all sounds that would be a distraction during the meditation.

How? 1. Begin by spreading out and finding a position that is thoroughly restful and comfortable. Close your eyes. In your mind's eyes, visualize your body. For five minutes, imagine that, one by one, all of the parts relax, with tensions and pressures in each part flowing out of your body as you exhale. Then imagine that you enter a building with one floor for each year of your life. Enter the elevator and press the button corresponding to the floor which you wish to visit. Imagine what that floor looks like; see the doorways, windows, furnishings and other details. Then meet God. What does God look like? Talk with God for as long as you wish. Say and do anything that you wish, and listen and watch as God responds to you. When you wish, return to the elevator and to your present. Allow some time to think about your fantasy experience. What are your feelings and thoughts and realizations?

If this is done as a group, someone is needed to read the directions slowly and meditatively. Allow the participants to close their meditation when they wish. When all have opened their eyes, you may wish to spend some time in sharing with each other anything you wish to say about your fantasy.

Suggested Reading

Bausch, William J. *Positioning Belief in the Mid-Seventies.* Notre Dame, Indiana: Fides Publishers, Inc., 1975.
An account of current theological thinking on such topics as belief, Christology, Church and dogma.
Bossard, James and Eleanor Boll. *One Marriage; Two Faiths.* New York: The Ronald Press Co., 1957.
Although this book operates with the old premise of the promises required of non-Catholics who married Catholics, the treatment of pressures on inter-faith marriages is realistic.
Fowler, James and Sam Keen. *Life-maps: The Human Journey of Faith.* Needham Heights, Massachusetts: Humanities Press, 1977.
A discussion of faith as personal growth, a life process.
Geissler, Eugene S. *There Is a Season.* Notre Dame, Indiana: Ave Maria Press, 1970.
An autobiographical approach to theologizing in the family setting.
Hendricks, Gay and Russel Wills. *The Centering Book: Awareness Activities for Children, Parents and Teachers.* Englewood Cliffs: Prentice Hall, Inc., 1975.
Both this and its companion volume (The Second Centering Book. Gay Hendricks and Thomas B. Roberts, 1977) give formats and suggestions for fantasy which you may wish to use as a basis for family prayer.

Keen, Sam. *To A Dancing God.* New York: Harper and Row Publishers, 1970.
A poetic exploration of life, values, and celebration in our times.

Kennedy, Eugene. *Believing.* Garden City: Doubleday and Co., Inc., 1974.
Discussion of the meaning of faith and believing, with a series of interviews with people from Ann Landers to B.F. Skinner on the subject.

Kung, Hans. *On Being Christian.* New York: Doubleday, 1976.
A thorough analysis of the implications of faith for today's Christian.

Moser, Lawrence E. *Home Celebrations.* New York: Newman Press, 1970.
A good variety of family prayer service scripts for home marking of important moments. Use these as patterns for your own services.

Piaget, Jean. *The Moral Judgment of the Child.* New York: The Free Press, 1965.
Scientific study of the changing processes by which children of various ages come to distinguish between right and wrong.

Pipkin, H. Wayne. *Christian Meditation: Its Art and Practice.* New York: Hawthorne Books, Inc., 1977.
A survey of methods of prayer; you may find it helpful for yourself and applicable to family prayer.

Pottebaum, Gerard A. *The Rites of People.* Washington: The Liturgical Conference, 1975.
An exploration of the nature and forms of ritual in our daily living.

Ryan, Mary Perkins & O'Neill, David P. *Moral Development, Sin and Reconciliation.* West Mystic, CT: Twenty-Third Publications, 1977.
A 4-step presentation for preparing children to receive the sacrament of Penance. Covers the nature of relationships, growth stages toward responsible maturity, basic questions on the sacrament, and analysis of Penance in our day.

Schmid, Jeannine. *Religion, Montessori and the Home.* New York: Benziger, Inc., 1969.
Patterns for using the young child's natural growth processes and interests as a basis for teaching about religious values.

Simon, Sidney. *Helping Your Child Learn Right From Wrong: A Guide to Values Clarification.* New York: Simon and Schuster, 1976.
Simon's techniques of values clarification which parents can use with their children in the setting of family discussions, mealtime games, and other occasions. The activities can be used as the basis for family prayers as well.

TeSelle, Sallie. *Speaking in Parables.* Philadelphia: Fortress Press, 1975.
Analysis of parable and poem, as well as autobiographical story, all as theology.

Evaluation

One of the factors that have advanced our work with families has been their willingness to share with us their reactions to our suggestions and their results when they try them. This questionnaire is enclosed in the hope that you will let us know how you fared with these suggestions, as well as what kind of materials would be helpful to you in the future.

1. Is this type of book helpful to you? _____ What sections appealed most to you?

2. Which of the Familylabs would you like to try?

3. With which ones have you had the greatest success?

4. What aspects of family living would you like to see developed in future books?

5. Are there family activities of your own design which you would like to share with us?

Send to: or to:
                                          Dr. Margot Hover
     Twenty-third Publications   Full Circle
     Box 180   4833 West 78 Terrace
     West Mystic, Conn. 06388   Shawnee Mission, Kansas 66208

Further information on related materials and/or lecture-workshops is also available.

About the Author

Professionally, Dr. Margot Hover, BA, MA, MRE, D.Min., has been a public and parochial school teacher, parish director of religious education, hospital chaplain, writer and consultant. She is presently Director of Full Circle, Shawnee Mission, Kansas, offering a variety of resources in communication and organization to businesses, churches, schools, and family groups. In her personal life, she has been a foster parent, and is presently known by the neighborhood youngsters as a friendly ear and a crack peanut brittle cook.